Front Cover: A view from the old Roxborough Bridge looking towards Harrow North signal box, as a mid-day LNER up train approaches Harrow on the Hill station in 1936. The rake of teak Gresley coaches is headed by a class B17 Sandringham no.2854 'Sunderland', whilst the daily Met coal train returns from South Harrow gasworks. It has travelled via the Uxbridge branch and emerges under the flyover, built in 1925 to reduce the conflicting traffic resulting from the opening of the Watford branch. The now mainly empty wagons, hauled by Met F class 0-6-2T no.91 in interim LT livery, are bound for the extensive Harrow goods yard on the left. *(Peter Green GRA)*

Inside Front Cover, top: The classic Met locomotive was the E class 0-4-2 tank introduced in 1896 which sustained their services over the Joint for many years, and even in the 1950's could often be seen as a reserve 'changeover' engine in the bay at Rickmansworth. No.L44 is seen here at Neasden LT before being withdrawn in 1963 and carefully restored as Met 1 at Quainton. *(Colour-Rail LT21/ J.H.L.Adams)*

Inside Front Cover, bottom: An ex-GC class 9P 4-6-0 'Earl Haig' in LNER green livery leaving Aylesbury for Marylebone heading an up Manchester express in 1938. Responsibilities at Aylesbury (Town) station were a matter of some complexity as it was shared between three companies, in the shape of the Met&GC and the GW&GC Joint Committees. *(Colour-Rail NE10)*

To my wife, Shirley

First Published 2000

By: Clive Foxell
4 Meades Lane,
Chesham,
Buckinghamshire   HP5 1ND

ISBN 0 9529184 2 0

Printed by: Stanley Mason Printers Ltd.,
61 Woodside Road,
Amersham, Bucks.   HP6 6AA

THE STORY
OF
THE MET & GC JOINT LINE

(OVER A HUNDRED YEARS OF SHARING A RAILWAY)

Dr Clive Foxell CBE FREng

" No Board has ever brought their shareholders a more valuable present
than we bring you today"

*Sir Edward Watkin, when making the announcement of the agreement to link the
Metropolitan and the Manchester, Sheffield & Lincolnshire Railways*

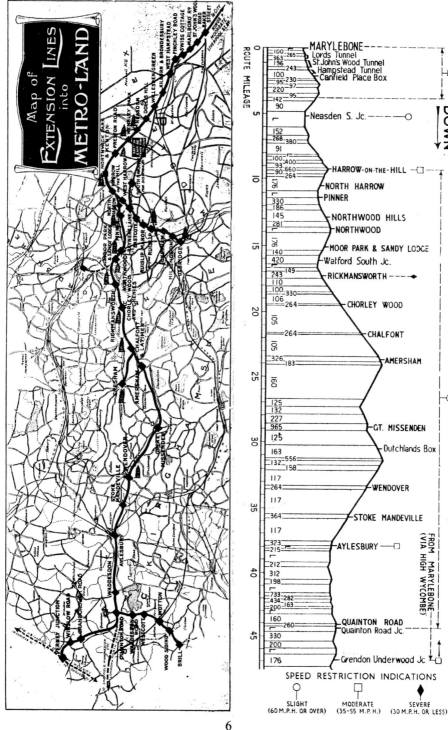

Map of
EXTENSION LINES
into
METRO-LAND

ROUTE MILEAGE

0

5

10

15

20

25

30

35

40

45

MARYLEBONE
Lords Tunnel
St. John's Wood Tunnel
Hampstead Tunnel
Canfield Place Box

DOWN

Neasden S. Jc.

HARROW-on-the-HILL

NORTH HARROW
PINNER
NORTHWOOD HILLS
NORTHWOOD
MOOR PARK & SANDY LODGE
Watford South Jc.
RICKMANSWORTH

CHORLEY WOOD

CHALFONT

AMERSHAM

GT. MISSENDEN
Dutchlands Box

WENDOVER

STOKE MANDEVILLE

AYLESBURY

FROM MARYLEBONE (VIA HIGH WYCOMBE)

QUAINTON ROAD
Quainton Road Jc.

Grendon Underwood Jc.

SPEED RESTRICTION INDICATIONS

SLIGHT
(60 M.P.H. OR OVER)

MODERATE
(35-55 M.P.H.)

SEVERE
(30 M.P.H. OR LESS)

6

PREFACE

The railway of the Metropolitan & Great Central Joint Committee was only 48½ miles in extent but, as I found with my earlier books on the Chesham branch of a mere 4 miles, length is no measure of interest. Indeed the 'Joint', as it was known by all those that worked on it, had an important role in railway history representing the peak in the career of that notorious and expedient Victorian entrepreneur and last 'railway king', Sir Edward Watkin, with his ambition to link Manchester and Paris by rail. Ironically, this was quickly nullified by the vacuum caused by his forced retirement due to ill health when acrimony arose over the sharing, by two of his erstwhile companies, of the railway between Harrow and Quainton Road. Finally, they reached an agreement in 1906 to operate this contentious line via a 'Joint Committee'.

It has been said that a classic story consists of 'a beginning, a muddle and an end' and this fits the history of the separately accountable 'Joint Committee' which operated from 1906 between the Metropolitan and the Great Central Railways, and finally London Transport and the LNER until 1948. Similar liaison arrangements for sharing the tracks continued with LT and British Railways and even today with Chiltern Railways. Inevitably this story reveals an anachronistic picture of an operating regime reflecting the completely different objectives, traffic, practices – and suspicions of the partners. It must have been confusing to work with the Joint where the different layers of management changed every 5 years! However, it had a special character all of it's own, which is well remembered and lingers on until today.

My own first experience of the Joint was before the last war as a boy on a fishing trip to the gravel pits at Rickmansworth. This involved travelling on a Met multiple electric train from Harrow on the Hill and changing at Moor Park to wait for a fast train hauled by a Met electric locomotive. At this time Moor Park station was a ramshackle affair built entirely from old sleepers. Suddenly a down LNER express from Marylebone headed by a 'Director' came into sight and everyone took cover as it thundered past causing the whole structure to shake to its foundations! Later I watched the trains at Harrow and in 1944 worked briefly as a casual cleaner at Neasden Shed. My career then occasionally took me via Marylebone station which still had a strong Great Central aura about it, for in the refreshment room one was served by waitresses in black & white uniforms who brought tea and toast on that distinctive heavy silver-like table ware, still emblazoned 'Forward'. Subsequently marriage took us to Chesham and the steam

'Shuttle' and since then I have been able to observe the electrification complemented by the launch of Chiltern Railways. Until recently 'Steam on the Met' reminded us of the great days of the Joint and the tremendous variety of traffic that it offered.

Another benefit of living in the Chilterns has been the ability to meet a number of people who had personal experience of the Joint either as members of the staff or as travellers. In this context I would like to thank all of them most sincerely, as well those mentioned below and the many others who helped me and without whom the creation of this book would have not been feasible. Nevertheless any mistakes that have occurred are entirely my responsibility.

Clive Foxell
Autumn 2000, Chesham

Acknowledgements

Book shops say that 'the cover sells the book', and in this respect I am most grateful for that well-known railway artist, Peter Green, in creating the atmospheric painting that appears on the cover. I am also indebted to that doyen of the GCR (and the Met), Richard Hardy, for his assistance and loan of some personal photographs, as well as other local railwaymen such as Bob Clarke, Eric Gane, Tony Geary, and Don Grant. Interest in the Joint has spread round the world and Jack Parnham in New Zealand and Patrick O. Hind in Canada have provided me with much useful material and advice.

Inevitably the related railway societies have given much assistance and I would like to highlight Michael Fish and the late David Jackson of the GCRS, Roy Miller of the Bucks Railway Centre, and the M&GN Photo Circle (together with Les Reason). Also the NMR, Michael Brooks for the photos by Stephen Gradidge, the LT Museum and the LCGB for providing photos from the Ken Nunn collection. In bringing the story into the present day John Scott of London Underground, Paul Spencer of Crossrail and Donald Wilson (Station Master of Marylebone) were kind enough to spare me their time.

It is said that "using only one reference is plagiarism, but using many is research" and most of the relevant documents are held at the London Metropolitan Archives and the Public Record Office. I am grateful to their staff for every assistance as well as those at the Bucks County Library (Local Studies) and the local libraries at Chesham, Chorley Wood and Rickmansworth. I am also grateful for the permission of 'The Railway Magazine' to reproduce some of their material. As always, local contacts have been extremely useful and my thanks go to Ron White (Colour-Rail), Richard Casserley, the late Tony Coldwell, Ray East, John Gercken, Peter Hawkes, Ken Goodearl, Jean Podbury, Ron Potter, Colin Seabright, Rodney Sedgewick & Trevor Wayman.

CONTENTS

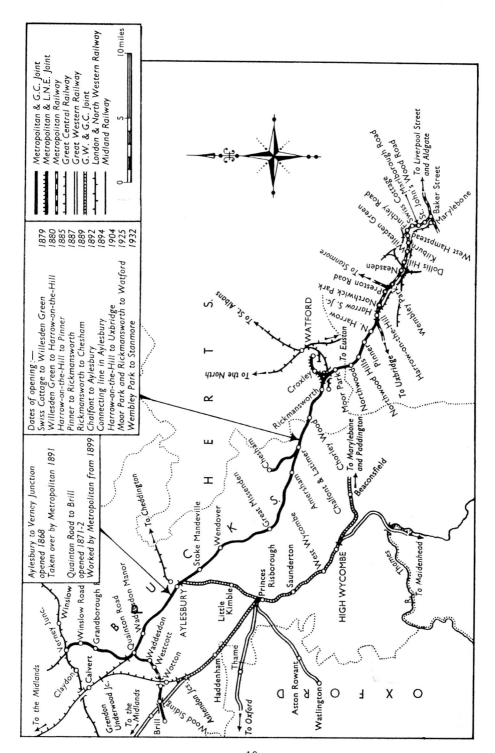

Metropolitan & G.C. Joint
Metropolitan & L.N.E. Joint
Metropolitan Railway
Great Central Railway
Great Western Railway
G.W. & G.C. Joint
London & North Western Railway
Midland Railway

Dates of opening:—
Swiss Cottage to Willesden Green   1879
Willesden Green to Harrow-on-the-Hill   1880
Harrow-on-the-Hill to Pinner   1885
Pinner to Rickmansworth   1887
Rickmansworth to Chesham   1889
Chalfont to Aylesbury   1892
Connecting line in Aylesbury   1894
Harrow-on-the-Hill to Uxbridge   1904
Moor Park and Rickmansworth to Watford   1925
Wembley Park to Stanmore   1932

Aylesbury to Verney Junction
opened 1868
Taken over by Metropolitan 1891

Quainton Road to Brill
opened 1871-2
Worked by Metropolitan from 1899

10

Chapter 1

From Little Acorns –

Perhaps it was as well that those in 1830 first proposing a railway to link the key northern industrial towns of Manchester and Sheffield did not realise that they were destined to become a pawn in the ambitions of Sir Edward Watkin. Yet this fate was to be shared with investors in another railway conceived to convey people between the burgeoning London railway termini and yet another in deepest Bucks. It would be difficult to find three more disparate railways in terms of location, purpose and length, but they did have greatness thrust upon them in the shape of Sir Edward Watkin.

The Manchester, Sheffield & Lincolnshire Railway began life in 1835 under the guise of the Sheffield, Ashton-under-Lyne & Manchester Railway, which was floated on the groundswell of enthusiasm created by the successful completion and financial returns of the nearby Liverpool & Manchester Railway – the first to rely on steam locomotives. The promoters were led by Lord Warncliffe, who appointed the eager Charles Vignoles as Engineer for the new line. He proposed a route of some 41 miles from Store Street in Manchester and finishing near the Cattle Market at Sheffield, representing a balance between minimising the problem of crossing the Pennines and accessing the nearby coalfields. Whilst using the valleys of the rivers Don and Etherow a challenging tunnel some 3 miles long at an altitude of over 900ft was still needed to reduce the approach gradients to a tolerable amount. The engineering was regarded as a daunting task but against the background of a rising stock market sentiment for railway investment the Act of Incorporation for the SA&MR was passed in 1837. Costs inevitably escalated and therefore Vignoles dropped some of the proposed branches and reduced the tunnel at the Woodhead Summit to only one line. Even so the revised capital requirement of £700,000 was subscribed in 1838. Track was started from either end of the line towards Woodhead where several shafts were sunk so that a number of tunnel headings could be worked at the same time. (One was to be used as the site for a signal box in the middle of the tunnel!) As time went on it became apparent that, whilst energetic, Vignoles lacked the organisational skill for such a large project. Unfortunately he was also under serious financial pressure as a consequence of investing heavily in the railway when the shares were at their peak. This led to his replacement by the more experienced Joseph Locke but nevertheless it took 6 years to complete the tunnel during which some 28 workers were killed and over

600 injured. It was finished in December 1845 and on the 22nd March the first train traversed the Pennines from Manchester to Sheffield, in some 2 hrs 10 mins.

By this time it was obvious to the directors that coal, other raw materials and the finished products would be the driving force in the growth of the SA&MR. Equally the outlet via the East Coast to the Continent would be just as important as that through Liverpool. Their desire to create an East – West trunk railway was against the reality that railway development was now becoming a more competitive, political and volatile business which focused the directors' minds on expansion by merger and acquisition. Thus, soon the Barnsley Junction Railway was absorbed whilst amalgamations with a number of other lines in the East gave access to Lincoln and the important fishing port of Grimsby. The latter was extended to New Holland, opposite to Hull across the Humber, bringing the length of SA&MR to over 200 miles and this led to consolidation in 1849, under the new title of the MS&LR. In the aftermath of the 'Railway Mania' the Directors now sought a fresh General Manager for the now sizeable railway and in 1850 appointed John Allport, who had risen from a clerk to senior posts in several northern railways. Having established an East – West backbone he moved to form links & running powers with the Lancashire & Yorkshire at Pennistone and with the Great Northern from Gainsborough.

John Fowler was now the Engineer and was responsible for major works that reflected the need of the MS&LR to bring their facilities up to match the demand. The first was the construction of an appropriate station at Sheffield (Victoria), followed by easing the bottleneck at Woodhead by driving a second bore and then creating suitable docks at Grimsby. Fowler went on to become a distinguished consultant whose name will occur several times throughout this story. Consolidation and efficient management in difficult times marked Allport's brief reign, which ended with his recruitment by the Midland Railway as their General Manager in 1853. His successor was an Edward Watkin, then of the London North Western Railway where he had been learning at the feet the machiavellian Captain Mark Huish, their General Manager.

Perversely, in the South the arrival of the railways just added to the existing congestion on the roads of London and by 1840 this was the limiting factor to the growth of the Metropolis. Not only did a large number of people live in the City but also it was the hub of a transport network supplying their needs – even ducks from Aylesbury were driven all the way to London, with their feet covered with tar and sand in order to protect them on the journey! In the town horse-drawn cabs, buses and carts predominated but as yet the roads were completely unsuitable and chaos reigned. Nevertheless as trade grew London attracted still more people, with the population doubling in 30 years: these required more horses which needed yet more horses to bring in the provender for them and remove the manure. This vicious spiral was accentuated in 1846 when a Metropolitan Railways Commission excluded mainline railway development from the centre of London and so the railways deposited their passengers on the periphery of the then City. By 1855 the congestion was intolerable and a Select Committee proposed easing it by an underground railway and major road improvements.

As we have noted at Woodhead, lengthy railway tunnels had been shown to be feasible, albeit if uncomfortable for passengers. But the catalyst for implementing the world's first underground railway was Charles Pearson, a City solicitor, who had long been concerned with the social consequences of the expansion of London. Indeed he had first proposed an underground railway in 1830 and inspired a railway promoter, William Mallins, to launch the North Metropolitan Railway. Unfortunately an economic depression plus the Crimean war destroyed confidence in such projects, but Pearson doggedly continued his campaign and persuaded the City Corporation to contribute £200,000 towards the required £800,000. To this the Great Western Railway also came forward with £175,000 on seeing the advantages of improving communication with their Paddington Station, which was then on the outskirts of London, and in ensuring that the new line would be laid with mixed-gauge track for their broad gauge trains.

John Fowler now reappears as the Engineer for the construction of this new Metropolitan Railway from Paddington to Farringdon, using the 'cut and cover' technique to build a tunnel under the New Road. Whilst Fowler received a fee of £137,700, a critical part of the work fell to his partner Benjamin Baker (with whom he was later to design the Forth Bridge) who successfully took responsibility for the tunnelling through the notorious consolidated clay which could exert dangerous lateral pressure on any workings. Pearson died in 1862, sadly just before the line opened in 1863. In view of public concern over the effect of smoke in such a confined space, an onus had been placed on the Met for their engines to 'consume their own exhaust'. To achieve this, Fowler commissioned a 2-4-0 'hot brick' broad gauge locomotive from Stephenson & Co but it was unsuccessful and the GWR had to be asked to provide some broad gauge engines.

Nevertheless smoke still created appalling conditions in the tunnels, but in spite of this the world's first underground railway was an immediate success and in the first year of operation it carried 9,455,168 passengers at a profit of £101,707. To build on this achievement the Met wanted to increase the frequency of the trains, however the GWR refused as they felt this would prejudice their own services to the City. The dispute hardened with the GWR threatening to withdraw their stock, but the Met stood their ground and just managed to carry on using borrowed stock from the GNR. The Met now went its own way by ordering some 4-4-0T condensing locomotives to a basic design from Beyer Peacock – these proved to be classic locomotives that sustained the Met into the next century.

Later the relationship with the GWR recovered to the extent that a joint western extension of the Met to Hammersmith was made in 1868, but the earlier dispute left a mark that was to be the trigger for a saga of ongoing disputes. To the east the Met pushed on to Moorgate in 1863 and Mansion House in 1871. At this time Fowler and some friends promoted an underground line as an independent spur from Baker Street (East) to Finchley Road, but it only reached Swiss Cottage in 1868. This failed to attract business and was of little consequence except that the Met provided the trains, and later gave them leverage for an outlet to the north.

Although the Met operations remained profitable, more capital was raised for the expansion and in order to mollify shareholders inflated dividends were paid out of capital and by other dubious devices. Some shareholders contested these actions in the courts and by 1870 several were pressing for a new Board of Directors. This agitation resulted in Sir Edward Watkin, now a established railway personality, joining the Board, then becoming Chairman in 1872 and bringing several of his trusty friends – such as John Bell from the MS&LR - as well as his ambition to link Manchester and Paris by rail.

Thus, two essential pieces of his intercontinental jigsaw were now in place and the stepping stone between them was to be provided by a somnolent single-track railway between Aylesbury and Verney Junction, in the middle of nowhere, on the LNWR line from Bletchley and Oxford. The Aylesbury & Buckingham Railway had been created in 1861 by two influential landowners and indefatigable railway promoters, the Duke of Buckingham and Sir Harry Verney. It relied on the former's presence on the LNWR Board for access to their existing station at Aylesbury but unfortunately the Duke's influence waned and with it any hope of a connection at Aylesbury. In their desperation, the A&BR turned to the GWR whose broad gauge line had already reached Aylesbury in 1863. At the cost of helping to pay for the GW to convert their track to standard gauge, the GWR agreed to allow the A&BR to share their station from 1868. The few trains that did run were provided by the GWR but were restricted to light engines in view of the state of the track. As these were of narrow gauge, and the GWR line to Aylesbury was still awaited conversion, the engines had to be delivered via Oxford and Verney Junction. Undeterred, in 1871 the Duke opened a private light railway some 6½ miles long from Quainton Road (on the A&BR) to Brill via Waddesdon Road, Westcott, Wotton, and Church & Wood sidings, on his large estate. This originally only carried his employees and goods but when it began to be used by local people the title of the Wotton Tramway was adopted – although the service was still provided by the same decrepit stock. Nevertheless, Watkin recognised their strategic significance with a presence in the Vale of Aylesbury and the involvement of his crony, the Duke of Buckingham. By 1875 Watkin got himself on the Board of the A&BR and so all the pieces of his jigsaw were in place. The next chapter describes how he attained such influence in the railway world.

(For simplicity, all the forms of the Metropolitan Railway are referred to as the 'Met', of the Metropolitan & Great Central Joint Committee as the 'Joint' and from London Passenger Transport Board to London Underground Ltd. as 'LT')

ooooO00Ooooo

The northern outpost of the Watkin empire centred on the MS&LR which built an impressive new station at Sheffield (Victoria) in 1851. This was the first station to be fitted with ticket barriers. In this scene in the early 1890's a new Parker 4-4-0 class 2 express engine waits in the relief road. (*Ian Allan/NRM*)

The London base for Watkin's ambitions was the underground Metropolitan Railway that had linked Paddington and Farringdon in 1863. In contrast to the idealised drawings in the Illustrated London News, this contemporary picture by Gustav Doré shows the reality of travelling on the crowded and sulphurous Met.

The excavation for the junction of the independent St. John's Wood Railway with the Met at Baker Street station. Because of it's poor prospects, the Met kept it at arm's length until Watkin found that his enemy, John Staats Forbes, thought that it might be extended to the north-west. This gave Watkin the idea of his 'Extension'. *(Illu. L. News)*

Looking for a route to the north, Watkin's eye also fell upon the Aylesbury & Buckingham Railway that had been built across the Vale of Aylesbury in 1868. The line from Aylesbury to Verney Junction included Winslow Road Station and this early photo shows the very basic single line laid with flat-bottomed rails. *(LT)*

During the life of the A&BR it borrowed light engines from the GWR and also shared the Aylesbury terminus of the GWR branch from Maidenhead, Wycombe and Princes Risborough. Looking south, the platform on the left was used by the GWR and that on the right by the A&BR. *(S Payne)*

The Duke of Buckingham was a major landowner in the Vale of Aylesbury and, as an enthusiast for railways, had helped to promote the A&BR. Subsequently in 1871 he built a light tramway from the A&BR at Quainton Road to go to Wotton, serving his estate. One of the first engines was this primitive Aveling-Porter no.1, prone to derailment.

In 1874 Baron Ferdinand de Rothschild started to build Waddesdon Manor. A temporary track was laid from the Brill Tramway to the hilltop site to facilitate the removal of spoil and the delivery of building materials, using horse-drawn wagons.

The Wotton Tramway was extended to Brill and began to convey passengers. By 1882 the Duke made a proposal to extend the line to Oxford as the Oxford & Aylesbury Tramway. Two Manning Wardle locomotives were acquired around 1890 to replace the earlier unsatisfactory engines and here 'Huddersfield' is at rest at Brill. *(Lens of Sutton)*

CHAPTER 2

THE RISE AND RISE OF SIR EDWARD WATKIN

Edward William Watkin, born in 1819, was the son of the prominent Manchester cotton merchant Absolom Watkin. His father gave Edward several advantages that were to propel him in his subsequent career – a wealthy background, access to influential people and a good Northern commercial background from working in his father's office. Also, significantly, a stirring introduction to the revolutionary possibilities of the railway when he was taken by his father to see the opening of the Liverpool & Manchester Railway. In spite of this help he was soon to make his own way for as a young man he involved himself in local affairs, becoming Director of the Manchester Athenaeum, literary works and founding the 'Manchester Examiner'. In 1845 he abandoned the cotton trade and became Secretary of the Trent Valley Railway, a line around Birmingham strategically placed in relation to the London & Birmingham Railway and others. He then contrived to sell the TVR to the emergent London & North Western Railway not only for a profit of £438,000 to his shareholders, but also on terms that the piratical manager of the LNWR, Captain Mark Huish, perceived to be favourable to himself! This balancing act well illustrates the abilities of Edward Watkin – business acumen, superb negotiating skills with tremendous flexibility to manipulate several options to achieve a personal objective, the ability to influence 'the great and the good' and being ruthless or affable as circumstances dictated.

Understandably Huish was impressed by the energetic young Watkin and persuaded him to become his Personal Assistant at the LNWR. Soon he was overloaded by the complex financial affairs of the Taff Vale Railway and had a breakdown which led to him being sent to America to recuperate. Watkin seemed almost to invite such crises by overwork and took pleasure in his ability to conquer what he deemed to be frailty. In 1851 he returned to Britain and the LNWR and two years later joined the MS&LR becoming their General Manager in 1854, where no doubt Huish expected him to collude with the LNWR. However Watkin was his own man and typically entered into a feverish round of complex negotiations with not only the LNWR, but also the Great Northern and the Midland Railways. However this was interrupted by a request from the Government to lead a mission to Canada to consider the formation of a Dominion of Canada, the feasibility of governmental control of the Hudson Bay Company and also the future policy towards railways in Quebec. On returning home he seized on the news that his MS&LR Directors had been negotiating privately with the MR and, realising that his future lay at Board level, took the opportunity to resign in apparent disgust. He returned to Canada to be Chairman of the Grand Trunk Railway, but two years later he rejoined the Board of the MS&LR, becoming Chairman in 1864 – a position he held until 1894. He married into a railway family and his first wife Miss Mary Briggs (d. Jonathan Mellor) who shared his enthusiasms and often accompanied him on railway visitations.

During this period when he was also Chairman of the South Eastern Railway and the Met where he undertook his most ambitious work, combining it from time to time with directorships of the GWR, GER, GNR and MR plus many other companies. In all this activity there was a common theme of a desire to facilitate – and therefore make a profit from – the international flow of goods by rail. This led to his participation in a new railway between Liverpool & Manchester, the very successful formation of the Cheshire Lines Committee, a proposed union of minor Welsh railways to give a much-needed North-South route from his empire around Liverpool to Cardiff, the Mersey Tunnel, Connah's Quay swing bridge, a railway tunnel between Scotland and Ireland and a canal between Dublin and Galway. He was also active in railways in Greece and, relevant to this story, in France. Knighted in 1868, he was created a baronet in 1880 and lost his wife in 1887.

Watkin was notoriously secretive about his intentions with investors, politicians and even with his colleagues, on the basis that if they did not know, then opposition would not be aroused! The abrasive side to his character was well in evidence when his Chairmanship of the MS&LR, SER and Met brought him into conflict with John Staats Forbes who was Chairman of the competing Metropolitan District and London Chatham & Dover Railways. Forbes presented a more polished image but their disputes were acrimonious, bitter, personal and obsessive to the extent of damaging their own companies. The central battles were over linking the Met and the MDR to form the 'Inner Circle' and the fight between their associated companies, the SER and LC&DR, for supremacy of the continental traffic from London to the English Channel ports.

Whilst these wars of attrition rumbled on, Watkin had his mind on the grand vision of a railway linking his Northern heartland of Manchester to his beloved Paris. Probably this idea arose from his early involvement in international trading, overseas railways, the stirrings for a tunnel under the English Channel and his Francophile leanings. Like all of his schemes he pursued it in secrecy, keeping several options open and advancing by increments that could be justified in themselves. With the MS&LR, Met (including access via the East London Railway through Brunel's Thames tunnel to New Cross) and the SER under his belt, all he needed to do in England was to close the gap between the Met and the MS&LR. As he also had influence over the Chemin de fer du Nord from Calais to Paris all that remained was a tunnel under the English Channel. The first geological survey had been performed by de Gamond in 1837 and a practical proposal for a Channel Tunnel followed in 1865 by the Submarine Continental Railway Co. (later the Channel Tunnel Co.) which was consolidated under Watkin's leadership in 1872. Excavations starting in 1881 between Dover and Folkestone, avoiding Forbes's LC&DR. Plans show lifts to lower the trains to the level of the tunnel and 4-4-0T engines similar to those on the Met with exhausts between the rails, where it was to be taken away by strong fans. Good progress was made using the new Beaumont tunnelling shield to cut through the chalk strata that was to be followed under the Channel. However Forbes felt that he had been sidelined and it is alleged that he lobbied the Army Chief of Staff, Sir Garnet Wolsely (immortalised by Gilbert as the 'modern Major-General') on the danger of the French army invading Britain through the tunnel. Watkin countered this with arrangements to mine and flood it in an emergency and earlier the French had even offered to build a spiral track at their entrance in order to give the British navy an improved opportunity for shelling any enemy trains!

But this was to no avail, and years of legal wrangling followed regarding Watkin's right to excavate his tunnel. Slow progress was made, often surreptitiously when Government inspectors were absent, and finally he claimed that he had manorial rights to the land – although he was unable to produce the documentation! Frustrated, work ground to a halt in 1891when some 2,100 yds had been excavated towards France and 1,800 metres in the opposite direction. Watkin never admitted defeat and lobbied his cause relentlessly in the House of Commons, where he had been an MP since 1857: even taking his friend Gladstone to his chalet on Watkin's newly-acquired Snowdon for indoctrination. His second wife was a Mrs Ingram aged 81 years, a wealthy widow, whom he married in 1893. This led to much gossip and although Watkin claimed to have 'ring-fenced' her fortune, there was no doubt that the Illustrated London News (which she owned) inevitably threw its weight behind his campaign for the Channel Tunnel.

In parallel with this saga, from the start as Chairman of the 'Sheffield' and the 'Met', Watkin had pursued an expansionist policy which led the MS&LR to be called the 'railway flirt' in the City. Pushing into North Wales via a bridge at Hawarden to Wrexham and Ellesmere, whilst to the East links were improved to the coast and to the North his eyes were set upon Blackpool. However his main objective was to the South and in typical fashion Watkin tried to advance on several fronts at the same time. Anxious to establish even a presence in London, by 1857 he had persuaded the GNR to give access to MS&LR trains over their tracks to London. Then whilst he continued discussions with the LNWR, GNR and MR to the extent of a possible merger, Watkin quietly extended the MS&LR from Sheffield south to Annesley, under the cover of accessing the North Derbyshire coalfield, but in reality to act as a launching pad for his new railway to join the Met in the South. And the man to implement it was William Pollitt, who had risen through the ranks to become his General Manager of the MS&LR.

ooooOOOoooo

CHAPTER 3

MIND THE GAP

Watkin perceived that it would be politically easier for the Met to break out from London than the MS&LR to break in. As Chairman of the Met, Watkin had been mainly embroiled in conflict with Forbes over an 'Inner Circle', but now seeking a way out of London to the North he realised that the anomalous spur of the semi-independent St. John's Wood line could now be exploited. It was Watkin's method to encourage local interests as a cover for his wider ambitions and then acquire them when the project matured. In this case the loose rein had a disadvantage in that his rival Forbes became an advisor and urged the St. John's Wood directors to seek powers to extend their line to join the MR and LNWR. However, the Met acquired control by exchanging 6% guaranteed Met stock and then used the powers gained by Forbes to establish an interchange for goods traffic with the MR at Finchley Road and push the railway onto Willesden Green by 1879. Watkin could now pontificate to his shareholders about the benefits that would accrue from 'The Extension' and began to hint openly about becoming a mainline railway to the North.

Beyond Willesden Green another local committee urging the case for a Kingsbury and Harrow Railway had been incorporated in 1874 and under their cloak the Met built the line on to Harrow on the Hill. Whilst the terrain was reasonably flat, it had involved a long embankment and major bridges at Kilburn and the over LNWR at Kenton. The station was central in Harrow and intended to be of a design compatible with such a place of learning and which no doubt reflected that the School owned some of the land. Consisting of two platforms, of which only one was used, the buildings on the north side were brick with stained glass windows & painted dados - said to be 'Queen Anne' style. It opened on 2nd August 1880 with a service of 36 trains per day and the Met's first goods yard received a coal train from the MR soon afterwards. The Inspectorate did not like the Met A class tank engines, which had no cab, running bunker first and insisted that a turntable was installed - but there is no evidence that it was ever used!

Although Watkin was not to know it, the Met line north from Harrow was later to become the Joint between two of his own companies. At that point however, he was still balancing his traditional options to advance - of building, acquiring or obtaining running powers. On one hand, he was still hoping for another railway from the Midlands being tempted to seek to use the Met as an entrée into London, then he could use them to forge a link with the MS&LR and thus avoid the expense of building his own line. Meanwhile an extension on to Rickmansworth was compatible with most options for the following moves:

1) A line to the south-west via High Wycombe, where this sizeable town had pleaded for connection to the Met.
2) A route along the Chess Valley via Chesham to Tring, joining the LNWR.
3) A direct route to Aylesbury, a major town, and the Vale beyond.

Therefore the Harrow and Rickmansworth Railway Bill of 1879 was deliberately vague as to it's real destination, but the Met contracted Maxwell to build the next phase under the direction of Charles Liddell as Engineer, who was privy to Watkin's thoughts. However Maxwell's financial position deteriorated and the Met was forced to take over responsibility. Construction was relatively straightforward except for the novel use of steel sleepers. Some unstable ground was encountered where the line crossed Lord Ebury's Estate and this would be an ongoing source of trouble. The intermediate stations were Pinner and Northwood, which opened with Rickmansworth in 1887. The stations were in the now standard Met design of two platforms with the offices on the north side. At Rickmansworth the two tracks ended at the turntable that had been moved from Harrow. The other feature was the location on a sharp bend resulting from the inability to acquire the desired land from the owner, John Finch who was Governor of the Bank of England. The Met was to rue the consequent speed restriction, which persists today. As might be expected from a town of about 1,000 people, the early traffic was disappointing, and only 561 passengers were carried to London in the first month. However freight such as coal and also gravel from Lord Ebury's pits began to grow.

By the early 1880's the Aylesbury destination was becoming more attractive because of a proposal to extend the Wotton Tramway from Brill some 11 miles into Oxford , as the Oxford & Aylesbury Tramroad. At once Watkin saw the possibilities of using the A&BR with connections to Verney Junction (and the LNWR), Quainton Road (nearer to the MS&LR) and now the prospect of reaching Oxford. Quickly he embarked on negotiations with both the A&BR and the O&AT (even getting the Met to pay for surveying the line to Oxford), whilst adopting a compromise route for the Met to join them at Aylesbury. In this he kept to the high ground to the future Chalfont Road so that he could first make a branch to the prosperous town of Chesham (pop.6,500) and then go on to implement an agreement he had struck with the LNWR to join their mainline at Tring. This would attract freight trains to the Met and potentially the Continent. Meanwhile at Chalfont Road he could continue his mainline above the Misbourne Valley, thus mollifying the notoriously difficult local landowners. The disadvantage was this was an inherently hilly route whose steep gradients added to later operational difficulties.

The attractions of Aylesbury as a target destination were increased when Liddell, who was already surveying possible routes across the Vale, discovered

23

Watkin's ambitious plans for a railway linking Manchester and Paris involved the South Eastern Railway, of which he was Chairman. In this photo of 1877 he is seen, in the centre wearing a smoking cap, with senior officers of the SER inspecting a slip of chalk near Folkestone Warren, whilst on his way to the site of his Channel Tunnel.

By 1880 the Met had reached Harrow on the Hill through open countryside and here one of their early A class Beyer Peacock 4-4-0T no.7 waits at the station. These engines had not needed cabs whilst working underground but, in spite of the exposed conditions over the Chilterns, it was some years before proper cabs were added.*(Ken Nunn/LCGB)*

This picture is believed to be of the first train at Pinner in May 1885. Staff pose with a highly polished A class Met engine and a set of rough-riding 4 wheel coaches. *(LT)*

The line was reasonably level beyond Harrow, with stations at Pinner and Northwood, where this photo was taken around 1900. The engine is a later version of the original A class 4-4-0T, a B class no. 59 which, after delivery by Beyer Peacock, had been loaned by Watkin to his SER for 3 years. *(LGRP)*

By 1887 the Met Extension had reached Rickmansworth and this scene shows no.45 of their ubiquitous A class tanks bringing a mixed rake of rigid 4 and 8 wheel coaches into the station past some typical Met signals. On the left is the water column that was wrongly placed and later had to be moved to the end of the platform. *(Ken Nunn/LCGB)*

Watkin kept his options open by pushing the Met on to Chesham - hopefully to join the LNWR at Tring, yet keeping to the high ground as far as Chalfont & Latimer to give alternative access to the Vale of Aylesbury. Here a contractor's engine is about to leave Chesham in early 1889 with some directors to inspect the work in progress. *(Ray East)*

A formal inspection of the completed line to Chesham took place on the 18th May 1889 complete with speeches and a banquet in the goods shed. This was the largest town on the Met route since Harrow and the local people were desperate for a railway service. This is a recently-found new version of the two well-known photos of the special train.

As his hope for extending the Chesham line to Tring fell through, Watkin drove the Met on from Chalfont Road towards Aylesbury. This is the traditional formal ceremony to mark the start of the construction with the turning of the first turf, at Stoke Road about ½ mile south of Aylesbury around 1891. *(Clive Foxell Collection)*

AYLESBURY RAILWAY.

FIVE POUNDS REWARD.

Some evil-disposed Person or Persons have lately *feloniously Stolen and carried away*, a quantity of RAILS, STAKES, and MATERIALS, belonging to the Company, for which any Offender, on Conviction, is liable to Transportation for Seven Years.

Several STAKES driven into the Ground for the purpose of setting out the Line of Railway, have *also* been *Pulled up and Removed*, by which a Penalty of Five Pounds for each Offence has been incurred, half Payable to the Informer and half to the Company.

The above Reward will be paid on Conviction, in addition to the Penalty, to any Person who will give Evidence sufficient to Convict any Offender guilty of either of the above Crimes, on application to Mr. HATTEN or Mr. ACTON TINDAL, of Aylesbury.

By Order of the Directors.

Aylesbury, August 18th, 1888.

May, Printer, Aylesbury.

No. 596.

METROPOLITAN RAILWAY.

NOTICE OF EXTRA TRAIN.

OPENING OF THE EXTENSION TO AYLESBURY.

Thursday, 1st September, 1892.

Special Train for Directors and others holding Cards of Invitation.

FROM LONDON.	Forward Special Train.	Empty, Light Train. Engine.
	A.M.	P.M.
BAKER STREET (EAST) ...	Dep. 10.47	5.47 ...
St. John's Wood Road ...	Pass 10.49	5.49 ...
Marlboro' Road ...	,, 10.51	5.51 ...
Swiss Cottage ...	,, 10.52	5.52 ...
Finchley Road ...	,, 10.53	5.53 ...
West Hampstead ...	,, 10.54	5.54 ...
Kilburn ...	,, 10.56	5.56 ...
Willesden Green ...	,, 10.58	5.58 ...
Neasden ...	,, 11.0	6.0	7.30
HARROW (Water)	Dep. 11.8	7.0	7.38
Pinner ...	Pass 11.12	Yard.	7.43
Northwood ...	,, 11.16	7.47
Rickmansworth ...	,, 11.22	7.53
Chorley Wood ...	,, 11.26	7.59
CHALFONT ROAD ...	Dep. 11.31	8.4
AMERSHAM ...	,, 11.36	8.9
GREAT MISSENDEN (Water)	,, 11.46	8.19
WENDOVER ...	,, 11.55	8.28
STOKE MANDEVILLE ...	,, 11.59	8.33
AYLESBURY ...	Arr. 12.05	8.40 Stop to Shed.

TO LONDON.	Empty Train.	Return Special Train.
	A.M.	P.M.
AYLESBURY ...		Dep. 4.20
STOKE MANDEVILLE ...		,, 4.26
WENDOVER ...		,, 4.32
GREAT MISSENDEN ...		,, 4.41 (Water)
AMERSHAM ...		,, 4.51
CHALFONT ROAD ...		,, 4.58
Chorley Wood ...		Pass 5.2
Rickmansworth ...	New	5.6
Northwood ...	Train	5.12
Pinner ...	from	5.16
HARROW ...	Yard.	Dep. 5.20 (Water)
Neasden ...	10.10	Pass 5.25
Willesden Green ...	10.14	,, 5.28
Kilburn ...	10.16	,, 5.29
West Hampstead ...	10.18	,, 5.31
Finchley Road ...	10.19	,, 5.32
Marlboro' Road ...	10.23	,, 5.34
St. John's Wood Road ...	10.25	,, 5.35
BAKER STREET (EAST) ...	10.27	Arr. 5.38

※ After the departure of the 10.29 a.m. Down train, the Engine of the 10.25 a.m. train into Baker Street to shunt 10.27 a.m. Up Special to admit of same Engine working Down Special train.

A.—The Up Aylesbury train due into Baker Street at 10.47 a.m. must be kept at St. John's Wood Road until 10.46 a.m.

B.—The Down train due into Willesden Green at 10.55 a.m. must be shunted to Up Line at once.

C.—The Chalfont Road Goods trains must be kept clear of above Special Trains.

※※ After the departure of the 5.39 p.m. Down train the Engine of 5.35 p.m. train into Baker Street to shunt 5.38 p.m. Up Special to admit of same Engine working Down Special Empty train.

E.—The Down train due into Willesden Green at 5.35 p.m. must be shunted to Up Line at once.

D — { On arrival of the Down "Special" at Aylesbury the Engine to run round and return with Empty Train to Stoke Mandeville and stand in Siding until 4.0 p.m.; thence to Aylesbury to form the Up "Special." }

GENERAL MANAGER'S OFFICE,
32, WESTBOURNE TERRACE, W.,
August 27th, 1892.

JOHN BELL,
General Manager.

Waterlow and Sons Limited, Printers, London Wall, London.

METROPOLITAN RAILWAY.

OPENING OF THE EXTENSION TO AYLESBURY.

SEPTEMBER 1st, 1892.

NOTICE TO THE STAFF.

On and after Thursday, 1st September, 1892, the Up and Down Lines between Chalfont Road, Amersham, Great Missenden, Wendover, Stoke Mandeville and Aylesbury, will be open for Traffic, and Trains will run at the times shown in the Supplementary Working Time Table issued to the Staff.

The following is a description of the Signals which will then be brought into use :—

Chesham was now to be on a branch as the new main line reached Amersham. The station was built on the hill above the existing town and was to the standard Met design. This shows the proud team of carpenters who were engaged in completing the goods shed. *(Clive Foxell Collection)*

Charles Liddell was the engineer for the Extension and used Joseph Firbank as the contractor. One of the engines he employed was 'Henry Appleby'. It is pictured above just north of Amersham around 1890 and was later used to haul an inspection train to Aylesbury for Sir Edward Watkin and other directors. *(Ray East)*

29

After the relatively easy route across Middlesex, the construction of the line over the Chilterns was more demanding. Here an embankment is under construction near Ostler's Wood just north of Amersham about 1890. The gravel required came from Chesham, Rickmansworth and excavations for Watkin's port at Dungeness. *(R East)*

The Met Extension opened to Aylesbury on the 1st September 1892, but due to disagreements with the GWR, it was not allowed to share their station and had to build a temporary one. This shows a group of Met employees gathered to welcome the first train. *(T Aslett)*

that the embryonic Stratford upon Avon & Midland Junction Railway would pass north of Quainton Road, through Moreton Pinkney (and nearer the M&SLR). This provoked Watkin to take pre-emptive action by getting permission from the Met Board to build their line on from Rickmansworth to Aylesbury whilst taking over the A&BR beyond. In typical Watkin fashion, he did this in 1891 by exchanging £158,500 of 3% guaranteed Met stock – before the Met reached Aylesbury. At the same time he made an agreement with the LNWR to use Verney Junction station based on sharing costs in proportion to their traffic. This left the Oxford & Aylesbury Tramway as an independent concern of the family of the Duke of Buckingham.

In 1890 Queen Victoria accepted an invitation from Baron Ferdinand de Rothschild to visit his new Manor House at Waddesdon and on the 13th of May she travelled by the GWR royal train, *"with a gaudily painted crown of iron at the base of the funnel"*, from Windsor to Aylesbury station. This was bedecked with decorations and surrounded by loyal subjects but, perhaps wisely, she eschewed completing the journey by the Aylesbury & Buckingham Railway via the Brill branch and used a horse-drawn coach instead. So when the Met took over the A&BR they built a new station at Waddesdon to serve the Manor.

Firbank was brought in again as the contractor for new line, double track to Chalfont Road and then a single line down the side of the Chess Valley to Chesham. The original terminus was to be about a mile out of Chesham but the local people bought land for the railway to end adjacent to the High Street (little knowing that Watkin had already bought land beyond this for the extension to the LNWR at Tring). Leaving the sharply curved exit from Rickmansworth the construction mainly involved cutting through the chalk of the Chilterns giving a ruling gradient of 1:105 through intermediate stations built at Chorley Wood and Chalfont Road, the former name being a Met invention and the latter by a clergyman of Chalfont St. Giles.

The gradient down to Chesham was mainly 1 in 66 and then the line curved over two bridges across the River Chess into the town, where the much-travelled turntable was re-erected. The service to Chesham in 1889 revolutionised this significant, but isolated, town and for two years it remained the farthest terminal of the Met. With a population of 6,500 it soon became a popular focal point for excursions. Soon after the opening of the line there was a major staff outing by over 3,000 employees of the Met at a fare of 1/- by special trains from Baker Street. Arriving about 3pm they marched behind the Harrow Town Band to the Park, and, although the weather was inclement, they watched their Met Staff Club play against the local Chesham Cricket Team. Later in 1892 some 250 people, including the choirboys of St. Mary's Church, paid 5/6 each to travel on the 6am train from Chesham to Brighton, returning home at 11.40pm. *"This they would have greatly enjoyed if they had not encountered torrential rain"*.

The success of the Chesham branch also revived the hopes that High Wycombe had long cherished for their own Met branch and in 1892 their Mayor and Chamber of Commerce again lobbied John Bell (now GM of the Met and ex-MSL&R) about the poor & expensive service provided by the existing GWR station. Bell arranged a special visit for them to Chesham including a fine lunch at The George, and thus encouraged commissioned a survey from J Wolf Barry of possible routes. He suggest a 12m railway from Rickmansworth either, northerly via Chalfont St. Giles, Penn Bottom and a 2,066 yd tunnel to High Wycombe or to the south via Chalfont St. Peter & Beaconsfield. It was reported to a 1896 Met Board that the first would be expensive and the second encountered unfavourable landowners in the shape of the trustees of the late Disraeli and a Mr Furnival – *"a lunatic estate in the hands of the Court"* – no action was taken but the episode did not help relations with the GWR.

The Chesham extension to Tring lapsed when Watkin's allies left the Board of the LNWR and he concentrated on completing the railway to Aylesbury via Great Missenden, over Dutchlands Summit (520ft) and down to the Vale through Wendover and Stoke Mandeville at a cost of £533,000. A station was opened in Aylesbury on the 1st September1892 to the traditional Victorian celebrations (wine was limited to a cost of 3/- per head: ie a bottle or so). Watkin, who was recovering from a stroke, led the proceedings with almost his usual energy and was accompanied by Sir Harry Verney now aged 93. But the event was also clouded by disagreement with the GWR who had refused to allow the Met to share their existing station. The GWR saw the Met acquisition of the A&BR as aggression and as well as refusing the use of their station withdrew their trains from the A&BR. Thus the Met was forced to build a temporary station and without any light engines to work the fragile track of the A&BR had to borrow some from the LNWR to maintain a service. Nevertheless it represented a considerable achievement for the Met who were now placed to provide a shorter & 20% cheaper route than the GWR or LNWR to London from such an important town. The traditional local trade in Aylesbury ducks boomed as a result of easy access to London and 'egglers' now collected large numbers of duck eggs from the vicinity for the London markets. However the intermediate stations were a different matter as illustrated by the report in a local paper: *"71 people booked on the first journey which left Aylesbury at 7.15 am and the great majority got out at Stoke and Wendover. For a village, Stoke may be said to have one of the largest and most comfortable stations to be found anywhere. In the event of their houses being destroyed by fire or flood, the whole of the inhabitants can be found shelter in the station building"*. Eventually relations were patched-up with the GWR and their station at Aylesbury was merged with that of the Met in 1894, becoming jointly owned with costs shared.

Although a major upgrade of the A&BR would be needed, the Met had now in theory reached Quainton Road and as the MS&LR prepared for the construction of new 93 mile line from Annesley to meet it, the realities of Watkin's scheme were beginning to become apparent. With his health deteriorating, Watkin tried to ensure that his satellites would comply with his grand design and in January 1890 all the main Boards under his Chairmanship passed similar resolutions, in effect 'swearing eternal allegiance and co-operation' to achieve this end. These minutes were signed by the respective General Managers and William Pollitt (MS&LR) with John Bell (Met) were delegated to prepare the requisite Bills for the creation of the London Extension. At this stage they readily worked together on this whilst Watkin masterminded the public and political campaign to win over objectors, of which there were many. The first group included the GNR who were annoyed over his disregard for their long-standing agreement over London working. Although they were appeased by the offer of reciprocal running rights on parts of the MS&LR, it stirred up a number of old foes that Watkin had affronted in the past. The other objectors were mainly provoked by the proposal to build a major new London terminus for the MS&LR at Marylebone, which had resulted from Watkin's belated recognition that Baker Street would not cope with the combined traffic. In this the main protests came from Lords Cricket Ground, under whose hallowed turf four tunnels were to be driven as well as the artistic community in St. John's Wood. The latter were not only worried about the demolition of nearby houses, but also the vibrations from the trains. Instinctively, Watkin realised that these were emotional issues which could sway public opinion and, as time was of the essence, he went to considerable lengths (with shareholder's money) to mollify both groups. The MCC ground was enlarged and even the local chimney sweeps were compensated for the lost houses. Late in the day the LCC tried to get the MS&LR to pay for a new road scheme around Marylebone and at this Watkin returned to his more robust demeanour.

In parallel with his parliamentary campaign, Watkin had been fighting an equally gruelling battle to raise the estimated £6.5 M capital for the venture. The Watkin empire had contributed token sums and therefore most had to come from shareholders, who were enticed by the prospect of a return of 6%.

In spite of strong support from Nottingham, Rugby, Leicester and other towns who believed that they would benefit, the first attempt to present the Extension Bill in 1891 was defeated. However the second Bill, which incorporated the revision needed for a terminus at Marylebone was successful, only to be delayed by a dissolution of Parliament so that the Act did not receive Royal Assent until 1893. Bell of the Met was already doubling and upgrading the line of the A&BR beyond Aylesbury to Quainton Road to meet the MS&LR, whilst Pollitt of the MS&LR placed the seven contracts for the matching sections South from Annesley. This line was the last steam era mainline to be built in Britain. It was to high engineering standards reflecting Watkin's ambitions of an express route in having a ruling gradient of only 1 in 176, avoiding sharp curves and to the generous continental loading gauge. Major works on the line were a number of fine bridges (including a 22 arch 180ft high viaduct at Brackley), major tunnels at Woodhouse, Catesby, Rugby & Woodford as well as massive excavations for traversing the built-up areas of Nottingham & Leicester. The construction benefited from the new technologies in civil engineering, such as mechanised excavators, and from contemporary photographs an excellent record exists in the book by Rolt. In addition, inserting a new terminus of optimistic proportions at Marylebone into a now well-developed London, added to the magnitude and cost of the task. However this peak of main line railway construction in the UK is not covered here in detail as it has been already dealt with extensively elsewhere.

In this Indian summer of his career Watkin was also pursuing his Channel Tunnel project, a new port at Dungeness and a Park at Wembley, complete with a copy of the Eiffel Tower. Under this pressure his health deteriorated rapidly and he was forced to resign all his Chairmanships in 1894. Ironically he had just witnessed the peak of his career in the ceremony to 'cut the first sod' of the London Extension near Lords, for although he remained nominally a director of the Met and the MS&LR, it was a sad figure that watched his empire disintegrate.

ooooOOOoooo

Chapter 4

The Poisoned Chalice

With the resignation of Sir Edward Watkin in 1894, a number of issues came together that had a profound effect on the future course of the Extension. The whole enterprise had depended on him for coherence of the loose association of companies which had the Met, MS&LR, SER and Channel Tunnel Co. as the core. Obviously the main impact was the loss of direction and single-mindedness due to the lack of a successor. It appears typical of 'one-man' companies that they are reluctant to grow a successor because they might oust them. This even seems to apply to close relatives – perhaps even more so. Nepotism was the norm in Victorian business and Watkin was no exception. His nephew Alfred Mellor was on many of his Boards, both of his wives were involved in his businesses plus relatives and a circle of cronies, but he rarely confided in them! Indeed his confrontational manner induced as much fear as respect in his associates. Therefore there was no obvious successor.

Ironically, just as he had learnt at the feet of the notorious Captain Huish of the LNWR, so his own managers had learnt from him and felt no obligation to collaborate with others within the 'empire' when it was of no benefit to themselves. In the case of Bell of the Met and Pollitt of the MS&LR, this was aggravated by a long-standing personal rivalry that went back to the time when they were both young clerks vying for promotion in the MS&LR. Now they were well-entrenched in their respective companies, which they regarded as their fiefdoms, and saw themselves vulnerable in any closer relationship with the other. Their sceptical view was reinforced when Watkin mooted a merger between the MS&LR and the Met – which would mean that one would have to work for the other! So what better stage to renew the contest between them than on the London Extension where there where certainly plenty of contentious issues waiting to be resolved?

In his concentration on propagating and securing his overarching vision of a trans-European railway Watkin tended to overlook practical aspects that got in the way. This is not to say that he was not interested in detail – indeed he often interfered – but overrode such considerations when it suited him. In particular he glossed over:-

1) The cost to the Met of upgrading the ramshackle A&BR to mainline standards, which involved relaying & doubling their track as well as replacing bridges, stations and rolling stock.
2) The cost of building the new MS&LR prestige mainline from Annesley to Quainton Road to European standards and the grand Marylebone station.
3) The relative commercial 'desert' traversed by this Extension.
4) The congestion that would result from MS&LR trains sharing the outer London commuter lines of the Met and the unsuitable terrain for their express trains.
5) The inability of Baker Street Station of the Met to cope with MS&LR trains and give access to the South Coast as proposed by Watkin. He had earlier vaguely mentioned that the MS&LR could have its own tunnel for their trains.

No doubt Watkin would have countered these criticisms by inferring that these were trivial points by comparison with the prize in view. However, to these underlying unresolved issues many more were to be added as the practical work began in constructing the London Extension of the MS&LR plus the upgrade to the Met. Apart from the threat of a take-over, Bell was concerned that the MS&LR could take part of his traffic away. Pollitt's sensitivity centred on the need to complete his line quickly in order to attract customers that would defray the interest payments on the loans to pay for the works. Therefore he saw Bell's subsequent actions as failing to implement the spirit of their Agreement of 1890 and expedite the access of the MS&LR to London. To add salt to his wounds, this first Agreement of 1890 (masterminded by Watkin) was particularly onerous on him, in that in exchange for allowing running powers for the MS&LR from Quainton Road to *Baker Street* the Met would receive 66 2/3% of their receipts.

As mentioned earlier, the Met had theoretically reached Quainton Road in the north in 1892 and work was now proceeding to upgrade the whole line from Baker Street station. The MS&LR Extension was moving rapidly south to join the Met and with it the late recognition that Baker Street was completely inadequate for all the envisaged traffic of both partners. Therefore a Bill was authorised in 1893 for a MS&LR line diverting from the Met via a tunnel at Canfield Place (near Finchley Road station) to a new major terminus at Marylebone. This was now intended to continue underneath the station hotel to connect with the Met west of Baker Street, thus giving access to south London. Soon some 3000 men were working on Marylebone with 1½ M tons of spoil being removed by the Met via three intermediate junctions with the old St. John's Wood Railway and taken out to a dump at Rickmansworth at a profitable rate of 1/- per ton.

The first big dispute concerned the precise track arrangements at Canfield Place. Watkin and Liddell, his engineer, had envisaged that the MS&LR would approach the Met from the *north* side, to allow it to later link with the LNWR, but Bell

The Met bought their D class light 2-4-0 tank engines in 1894 to replace those that they had hired from the LNWR to work the recently acquired A&BR line. But these were not a success and were soon relegated to light goods work and the Brill branch. Here no.71 of the class works a mixed load near Waddesdon in 1916. *(Ken Nunn/LCGB)*

The long-lived Met E class 4-4-0T's were introduced from 1896 to take over the increasingly onerous Extension duties from the valiant A class engines. Here two pass near to Chorley Wood. They proved worthy successors and continued to stand-in up to the 1950's. *(Colin Seabright)*

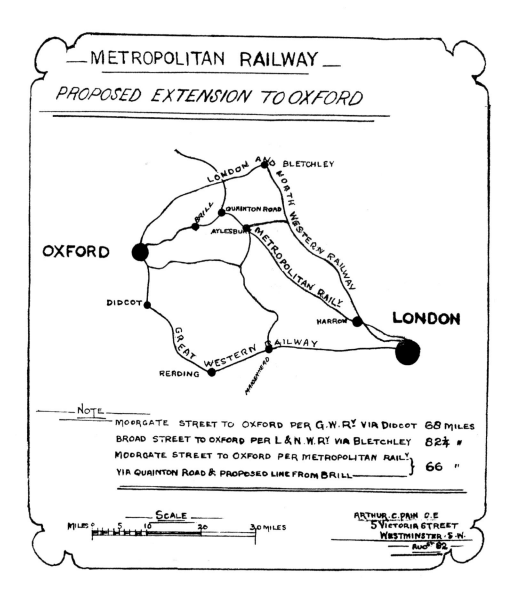

METROPOLITAN RAILWAY

PROPOSED EXTENSION TO OXFORD

BLETCHLEY

LONDON AND NORTH WESTERN RAILWAY

BRILL

QUAINTON ROAD

AYLESBURY

METROPOLITAN RAILY

OXFORD

DIDCOT

HARROW

LONDON

GREAT WESTERN RAILWAY

MAIDENHEAD

READING

__NOTE__

MOORGATE STREET TO OXFORD PER G.W.RY VIA DIDCOT 68 MILES

BROAD STREET TO OXFORD PER L&N.W.RY VIA BLETCHLEY 82¾ "

MOORGATE STREET TO OXFORD PER METROPOLITAN RAILY } 66 "
VIA QUAINTON ROAD & PROPOSED LINE FROM BRILL

__SCALE__

MILES 0   5   10   20   30 MILES

ARTHUR.C.PAIN C.E
5 VICTORIA STREET
WESTMINSTER·S·W·
AUGST 82

A contemporary map of the survey prepared for Sir Edward Watkin, and paid for by the Met, of the proposed extension of the Oxford & Aylesbury Tramway from Brill to Oxford. The 'note' contains some selective comparisons of the attractiveness of this route in relation to the competitors.

THE NEW
MANCHESTER, SHEFFIELD AND LINCOLNSHIRE RAILWAY EXTENSIONS.

CAUTION!

Before Sanctioning or Aiding any further increase of traffic over the London Metropolitan and District Lines, all Peers, Members of Parliament and other influential authorities, especially Ministers responsible for procuring the Royal Assent to measures seriously affecting the lives and safety of Her Majesty's subjects, are earnestly requested to read

"FACTS FOR SHAREHOLDERS,"

SHOWING THE

Critical Condition of the Underground Railway,

AND THE

EXTRAORDINARY DISCLOSURES ! ! !

CONTAINED IN THE

SUPPRESSED REPORTS

OF

William Booth Scott, Esq., C.E.

(30 Years Chief Surveyor to the Borough of St. Pancras),

As to the extraordinary and dangerous Sinking of the Tunnel in Euston Road.

Presented to the Highways, Sewers, and Works Committee at the Public Meetings held at the Vestry Hall on TUESDAY, December 14th, 1886, and TUESDAY, May 11th, 1886, but never submitted to the Shareholders at any of the subsequent General Meetings of the Railway Company.

TAKEN IN SHORTHAND, by Mr. THOMAS CANNON,

GREAT CENTRAL RAILWAY.

Circular No. 5072.

For the information of the Company's Servants only.

OPENING

of the

London Extension Line

for

COAL TRAFFIC,

JULY 25th, 1898.

GOODS TRAINS.

Explanation of References.

A Will stop to attach only	M Mondays excepted
D Will stop to detach only	M O Mondays only
R Runs when required	S Saturdays excepted
T Will stop for tracing only	S O Saturdays only
T D Will stop for tracing or to detach	W Will stop for water only
X Will stop when required	

The following Coal Train Service will come into operation on Monday, July 25th, 1898.

($\frac{133}{113}$)

Metropolitan and Great Central Joint Committee.

RULES AND REGULATIONS

FOR THE GUIDANCE

OF THE

OFFICERS AND MEN

IN THE SERVICE OF THE

METROPOLITAN AND GREAT CENTRAL JOINT COMMITTEE.

JULY 1st, 1920

LONDON,
WATERLOW AND SONS LIMITED, PRINTERS, LONDON WALL.

The GCR laid 'the last main line' from Annesley to Quainton Road in 1896 and, after much Met prevarication, it opened to their grand new terminus at Marylebone on the 9th of March 1899. Above, the first train is arriving at Brackley station, which was built to a standard island design used by the GCR for most of their intermediate stations.

By 1902 the preparations had begun to provide separate tracks for the GCR at Harrow to ease congestion. As a Met E class tank no.70 for the wilds of Verney Junction eases into Harrow, the widened Station Road bridge can be seen in the background which would accommodate new tracks for the Met on the left. *(Ken Nunn Collection/LCGB)*

Although Harry Pollitt had by now been replaced by Robinson, it was his locomotives that had to bear the brunt of hauling the new GCR London expresses. His class 11A 4-4-0 engines were often employed in these early days when trains were lightly loaded and here no.870 heads an up express near to Northwood.*(David Jackson Collection)*

Pollitt had designed some elegant 4-2-2 locomotives specifically for the fast Marylebone services. Here one of the 7ft. 9in. single-wheelers, no.968 of his class 13, heads a down express past Northwood on the Met. The train consists of a newspaper van plus a rake of Parker coaches. *(David Jackson Collection)*

This picture epitomises the failure of Watkin's grand ambitions. At Wembley over the hill lies the Met - now at loggerheads with their erstwhile partner the GCR, whilst on the hill stands his forlorn rival to the Eiffel Tower - representing his hopes for a railway to Paris. And in the foreground the construction of the GC- GW line to bypass the Met.

Early days under the new regime of the Joint Committee in 1906. A group of Chesham station staff pose at the end of the platform in front of a fine Met starter signal and a water crane. On the far left wearing caps are the booking office clerks James Woodward and to the right, 'Tug' Wilson. *(Jean Podbury)*

countered by claiming that it had never even been discussed at his Board (*"you are under a mistake that any arrangement was ever come to with this company"*) and stated that it must be laid on the *south* side. Then with a due show of reluctance (*"we are strongly impressed with the necessity of our own line to Wembley"*) then Pollitt agreed, as it would suit the MS&LR better in the long term to bypass the already overloaded Met and also build the needed new engine shed on this side of the tracks at Wembley. However this southern approach led Pollitt to ask that the existing West Hampstead Met station should be slewed to the north to give room and this became intertwined with his proposal to create a joint interchange station at Willesden Green which could have benefits for both parties, but Bell felt that the balance would be against the Met and he avoided real action on the project.

From this point, as Pollitt tried to force the pace, Bell employed every form of delaying tactic from avoiding replying to letters, asking for pedantic clarifications, arguing about the interpretations of the 1890 Agreement and then litigation – to obstruct the MS&L. As a consequence of Bell's prevarication over the junction with the Met, without any warning Pollitt slyly introduced a bill in the 1895 session to authorise a new railway from Canfield Place running parallel to the Met and joining it at Harrow South. As might be expected Bell regarded this as breaking the Agreement in bypassing the Met and launched a vociferous counter-attack. Legal arguments flowed but with the mounting pressures to finish the line bearing down on Pollitt he reluctantly agreed to a compromise which was enshrined in the MS&LR Act of 1895. In this the Met agreed to build this line from Canfield Place to Harrow South and grant a lease to the MS&LR for their exclusive use on condition that they did not pickup passengers or goods in between. (A clause also gave the MET the right to access across these new tracks to their sidings and Watkin's Tower at Wembley.) Although work soon started on these adjacent lines, they were not opened for traffic until 1901 and a temporary junction was built at West Hampstead in 1895 to allow the MS&LR trains to join the Met tracks. Bell also craftily persuaded Pollitt to give up his plans for a loco depot at Wembley and instead sold him some of the surplus Met land at Neasden for this purpose.

Two events were now to disrupt the possible truce between Bell and Pollitt and these would throw a long shadow over the future shape of their railways. One arose in 1897, just as the MS&LR had formally adopted the title of the Great Central Railway to reflect their enlarged domain. A decision was now becoming urgent on finalising the short underground connection from Marylebone to the south via the Met Inner Circle line to the west of Baker Street. Bell was at first evasive on the practicalities of the scheme and when pushed for clarification made conditions that were blatantly unacceptable to Pollitt. These would have restricted the GCR trains to only operating at night, with Met locomotives and at questionable charges. This attitude of Bell forced the GCR to look for an alternative solution for obtaining access to the south and thus they came to the conclusion that it would be preferable to avoid the rail congestion of inner London altogether. As the GCR now passed relatively near to the GWR an ideal exchange point would be at Banbury and negotiations were started with that old enemy of the Met.

By 1st January 1897 the Met had completed upgrading and doubling of their ex-A&BR track from Aylesbury to Quainton Road and this allowed Bell to make a pre-emptive strike. He suggested to Pollitt that the Met could now extend their line north some 24 miles to meet the GCR at Morton Pinkney. This place occurred earlier in our story when Watkin saw it as a staging post in joining other railways in the Midlands to reach Birmingham, and now in nominally seeming to help the GCR, Bell had similar ideas for his own benefit. However Pollitt needed the line as quickly as possible and did not want to rely on the tardy Met, so he deflected Bell's offer by insisting on onerous financial conditions that he knew would be unacceptable.

These events helped to convince Pollitt that Bell was a reluctant partner and so the GCR turned to negotiate with the GWR for better access to London. The latter were already seeking a shorter route than from Paddington to Birmingham via Oxford in order to compete better with their LNWR rivals. By extra powers in their Act of 1896 the GWR were already entitled to construct a line from Old Oak Common (near their depot by Paddington) to High Wycombe and upgrade their existing line to Princes Risborough, where it was already linked with the Met at Aylesbury. The GCR now realised that they might bypass the congested and tortuous Met route and prepared a bill in 1898 that effected this by a line from Neasden to Northolt (which was on the new GWR tracks). This move had not been mentioned to the Met and, realising that they had been outflanked, inevitably raised vociferous objections in claiming a breach of the spirit of their 1890 Agreement. The GCR countered by pointing out how the Bell's intransigence had interfered with the progress on the objectives of the Agreement and forced them to take alternative action. Thus, Parliament passed the Bill for the Neasden – Northolt line but recognised an injustice had been done to the Met and ruled that they should be compensated for any nugatory expenditure and diversion of traffic.

This only exacerbated the relations between the two parties. Pollitt desperately wanted to complete the GCR and generate revenue – he was already faced with interest payments on loans running at over a £1,000 per day and had to obtain the rolling stock for the Extension by hire purchase. Bell continued his policy of non co-operation by working to the letter of the Agreement and more disagreements on operational matters arose as the opening of the line drew near. Typical disputes were: -
- The cost of the telegraph installation.
- The adequacy of the Met track for the heavier & faster GC trains.
- Siting of coal depots.
- Provision of a shed for GCR banking engines at Aylesbury.

- The adequacy of the Met signalling system.

Bell was deliberately evasive in providing the necessary information to Harry Pollitt (MS&L Locomotive Engineer & son of William Pollitt) on line gradients, curves and clearances. Meanwhile Harry Pollitt was particularly concerned about completing the new GCR engines he was constructing for the Extension. Trying to progress matters, in 1897 he sent Bell drawings of the dimensions of the GCR engines, but Bell ignored these and asked for the gauge of their coaches. Harry Pollitt did this, but commented that *"running a train at a fair rate of speed is the only satisfactory mode of gauging"*. However when the Met drawings were made available they revealed that height clearances were insufficient for GCR stock on the Finchley Road – Chesham route and that significant civil work was necessary.

The dispute over banking engines arose over the desire of the GCR to have banking engines available at Aylesbury to assist their trains up the 1 in 117 past Wendover and surreptitiously they acquired land for the purpose, but Bell refused to allow it to be connected to the mainline! By the June of 1898 the GCR inspection of the Extension concluded that coal traffic could commence in a month in order to consolidate the track and that normal goods trains could follow in a few weeks. However Bell continued to prevaricate by refusing to allow any meetings to set the necessary timetables for these trains, on the grounds that the GCR line was not yet complete in every detail. Pollitt responded with a precise legal rebuttal and the test runs then took place, but encouraged by his success he took a step too far by trying to run a coal train just before the agreed time on the 25th July. An incandescent Bell leapt into action and appeared at 3am at Quainton Road signal box to order his signalman to stop the invading GCR train, which was forced to reverse! Ironically, as agreed, a few hours later the first GCR coal train traversed the Extension. But again Pollitt unwisely pushed his luck by proposing to run a coal train on to the GWR via Aylesbury in order to avoid the 'old' Met. Bell was just within his rights to refuse this but as usual the matter went to court and it further soured relations at a critical time.

On the 7th November 1898 the first passengers, albeit senior GCR officials, were conveyed into the new Marylebone Station and the formal grand opening took place with proper pomp and ceremony on the 9th March 1899. This included three special trains from Manchester, Sheffield and Nottingham that used the Met Extension and public services began on the 15th March.

Another issue arose from the anomalous role of the rustic Wotton Tramway that had been transmuted into the O&AT as part of the earlier machinations of Watkin and was now somewhat out on a limb. The current owners were led by Earl Temple (a descendant of the Duke of Buckingham) who approached the Met in 1899 to seek absorption into their only link with the outside world. However the Met declined the request for payment of £20,000, as the GCR would not contribute, but then agreed to operate the line in exchange for paying a rent of £600 pa to the O&AT.

A combination of these ongoing disputes and the outstanding issue of recompense to the Met for the GCR & GWR manoeuvres led to the invoking of the arbitration clause of the original 1890 Agreement. However the GCR were now in a stronger position for it had continued negotiations with the GWR to extend as a joint venture the line from Northolt Junction to Princes Risborough and then north to Ashendon, where the GWR would go on to Birmingham. But from Ashendon the GCR could then build a short connecting line to Calvert on their mainline thus giving access via the new well-graded track to their terminus at Marylebone, which completely avoided using the Met. This GW&GC Joint Committee line, including the right to compensation for the Met, was enshrined in their Bill of 1899.

Lord Robertson was appointed as the arbitrator but it needed changes in the leading characters to ease the situation before a conclusion was reached. The new Heads of Agreement were available in 1904, becoming an Act in 1905 and then implemented in 1906, with the effect of creating a Met & GC Joint Committee responsible for the shared line from Harrow to Quainton Road. Any hope that this ruling would end all disputes between the two companies was doomed to be premature for, as we shall see, circumstances changed and such a complex document would be capable of divergent interpretations – to the end of the Joint.

However, as the century came to an end the GCR were now running their own trains over the Met via Quainton Road. These included the early morning newspaper distribution train from Marylebone which, in different guises, ran until 1967.

ooooOOOoooo

CHAPTER 5

THE OLD ORDER CHANGETH

With GCR trains now running over the Met the new century was to usher in a radical change in the cast of players that had been involved in creating the contentious Extension. At almost the beginning of this saga Edward Watkin had been knighted in 1868, becoming a baronet in 1880, but now as an invalid in a wheelchair witnessing the opening of Marylebone many conflicting thoughts must have passed through his mind. Although revered as "the grand old man of the late Victorian railways", his behaviour had created serious reservations in the City to the extent that the share prices in his companies rose when he retired. On one hand he had built and acquired numerous railways – including the "last mainline" in Britain - but he also left behind the shattered dream of an intercontinental railway. He died shortly afterwards in April 1901.

His onetime trusty lieutenant William Pollitt, who ran the GCR, had been knighted in 1899, but his aggressive stance had alienated his own Board and he became increasingly sidelined and sought retirement in May 1901. By this time Alexander Henderson, the financier who by his efforts in the City had virtually kept the GCR solvent in recent years, was running the company and was soon made Chairman. Immediately he recruited as Pollitt's successor Sam Fay who had resuscitated the moribund Midland & South Western Junction Railway. This was a brilliant choice, for as General Manager he was a charismatic and entrepreneurial leader who sought to put the company on a sound footing by attracting business to exploit the new routes of the GCR created by the Extension. To do this he assembled an outstanding team including John George Robinson as a new CME (to replace the enigmatic Harry Pollitt), Dixon Davies as the Solicitor, A F Bound as Signal Engineer and Messrs.Dean & Dawson to create a marketing arm. Under Henderson, soon to be Lord Faringdon, dealing with finance and strategic matters they succeeded in revitalising the GCR and most of them remained with the company until overtaken by the Grouping of the railways in 1923.

On the other side of the fence changes of equal significance and nature were also taking place at the Met. Bell as their intransigent Chairman & General Manager became ill and had to retire in 1901 when he was replaced in his role as Chairman by Col. John Mellor (a brother-in-law of Edward Watkin!). However, this overhang from the previous era only lasted until 1904 when the future Lord Aberconway took on this role. Abraham Ellis the Company Secretary had taken over as General Manager, but it was a Robert Selbie who replaced him as Secretary and became General Manager in 1908 and the driving force at the Met. Both of the new teams at Met and the GCR inherited a shared Extension line in a manner that neither would have wished, but both sides approached the problems in a pragmatic way without carrying the baggage of personal animosities of their predecessors. Progress could now be made to try to resolve the serious practical issues arising from the aftermath of the original 1890 Agreement.

The GCR rapidly hit their stride in operating the Extension and although the passenger traffic started lightly, the level of goods traffic was most encouraging. From the 31st July 1901 they had exclusive use of the new tracks parallel to the Met from Canfield Place to the junction at Harrow South, thus avoiding this increasingly congested sector of the Met. By 1903 a pattern of services had been established with 11 down express trains from Marylebone to the north, of which one was the early morning newspaper train and 8 of the others included luncheon/restaurant cars for which the best time to Manchester (London Road) was 4hr 17mins.. The up service was similar and in addition there were 8 semi-fast trains which covered the journey from Aylesbury in 59 mins.

However progress was also being made towards bypassing the Met altogether with the GW&GC Joint line. From August 1901 GCR heavy fish and goods trains had accessed London from the north via Aylesbury, Princes Risborough, & Maidenhead to the GWR main line and the south. But on 1st August 1905 the GW&GC Joint line was ready to handle goods trains. It was formally opened from Marylebone on 2nd April 1906 and soon Fay began to switch some of his express trains to the new route with ambitious schedules. However his new CME, John George Robinson had inherited an inadequate stock of locomotives for this new main line. His predecessor, the enigmatic Harry Pollitt, had been dogged by difficulties in producing enough new engines and then maintaining them, and as other UK construction capacity was lacking, he was forced to buy some from the USA. He continued to build earlier designs of Thomas Parker and designed some new 7ft.9in. 'singles' & 4-4-0's with 7ft. coupled wheels for the Extension, but these were not delivered until after he was effectively asked to resign in 1900. Robinson borrowed some locomotives from other companies to supplement these deliveries and started to rebuild existing Sacre, Parker and Pollitt types. But his main thrust was to create a new range of basic engine types that would be evolved to sustain the GCR into the future. The first was the robust class 9J 0-6-0 locos desperately need for freight work, followed by a foretaste of Robinson's stylish touch in the elegant 11B 4-4-0 express, the class 8 4-6-0 express goods for fish traffic, the 8A 0-8-0 mixed traffic and the 9K 4-4-2 tank locos for commuter trains. These were complemented by coaching stock for the new long distance services, although for expediency Thomas Parker Jr. (Carriage & Wagon Superintendent) first bought coaches from outside suppliers to ease the situation.

These were followed by new designs that set high standards for elegance and comfort. With their Gorton Works working to capacity and the tremendous pressure for more wagons, orders had to be placed with outside suppliers.

The Met also devoted resources to developing its 'main line in miniature'. Track clearances had been increased to comply with the more generous dimensions of the GCR (& others) and over 8 miles of the original steel-sleepered track was replaced between Northwood and Great Missenden. With their increased catchment area the potential for freight traffic that Watkin had envisaged began to be exploited and an investment was made in 250 new wagons. Equally, during the past 25 years passenger traffic had more than doubled to over 90 M carried in the year. At the completion of the Extension most Met trains were hauled by the original Beyer Peacock A&B class 4-4-0T locomotives which, although performing admirably over the Chiltern Hills and being retrofitted with cabs, had been intended for the confines of the Inner Circle. The associated passenger stock was still the primitive and rough-riding rigid wheelbase coaches that gave much cause for complaint.

The first Met engines built specifically for the longer journeys were 4 of a C class 0-4-4T in 1891. As the Met was never of a size to justify a significant production of locomotives within their own works, they tended to procure them from outside suppliers. In this case Neilson's made them to a design based on Watkin's SER Q class engines. When the Met absorbed the A&BR line to Quainton Road and Verney Junction it was being worked by light engines loaned from the GWR and this continued until disputes with between them led to their withdrawal in 1894. In this emergency the Met borrowed similar locomotives from the LNWR until two of the D class 2-4-0T's, similar to a Barry Railways design, were obtained by the Met from Sharp Stewart. Unfortunately these were not a success and they were soon relegated to light goods duties.

Newer coaches with proper bogies were bought from Ashbury around 1899 which were complemented by an enhancement of the earlier C class engines in the form of 7 of the shapely E class 0-4-4T locomotives, by T F Clark from Neasden Works and also Hawthorn Leslie, around 1901. These classic engines, which for many came to epitomise the Met, formed the backbone to their passenger services whilst the growing freight operations were handled by 4 new F class 0-6-2T's supplied by the Yorkshire Engine Co. With these two types of engine providing the mainstay, a basic pattern of services was established that continued for the life of the Met. Selbie had also recognised the significance of the electrification of London commuter lines and by November 1905 the Met was operating their electric trains out to Harrow and then over their new branch to Uxbridge. Now, apart from goods and service trains, the changeover from steam to electric traction was made at Harrow.

With this improved access to London the area covered by the Met was now developing rapidly and attracted a number of 'well to do' people to move into the area thus adding to the existing relatively high proportion of 'landed gentry'. Typical of these was the Rothschild clan, where Baron Ferdinand commenced building his chateau on top of a hill at Waddesdon with the assistance of a rail link to the site from the nearby Brill tramway. Other members of the family created stately homes each at Ascott, Aston Clinton, Eythrope, Halton, Mentmore & Tring. Rail was a preferred form of travel and Baron Ferdinand even had his own saloon carriage built in 1905 for 'specials' or attachment to Met service trains. As a consequence these establishments, with their need for victuals and their armies of servants, generated considerable traffic for the Met. On Sundays the local stations would be thronged with servants off on a day trip to their relations.

They also attracted high profile visitors who boosted the status of the railway; however such occasions could also have their downside. Prince Edward was a frequent guest to friends in the locality for his 'assignations' and in July 1898 he had fallen on the stairs at Waddesdon Manor and broken his leg. Then whilst being carried in a chair over the footbridge at Aylesbury station the seat collapsed, leaving the Prince on the ground only to be enveloped in a cloud of soot from the engine beneath! Things went better on 16th January 1902 when a special Met train took the now King Edward VII in the evening from Baker Street to Amersham to visit Lord Howe at Penn. The journey only took 36 mins for the 24 miles and most of the Officers of the Met were on hand to ensure all went correctly. The MS&L did not fare so well in 1901 when the King was returning from a trip to Leopold de Rothschild via Wendover and to his intense displeasure the train arrived some 10 mins late at Marylebone. He left the assembled MS&L top brass in no doubt about his feelings.

However the cause of this delay was symptomatic of the current difficulties of a shared line without overall control, for a Met pick-up goods train meandering from station to station had been allowed to precede the Royal train. Another incident in 1905 further illustrates this problem. A passenger arrived by cab late at Marylebone just missing his favourite midnight train back to Aylesbury. Desperately wishing to get home he asked for a special train which was provided, at a cost of 5 guineas, and directed to run fast to Aylesbury. When it approached Chorley Wood the signalman gave it priority over the earlier train that the gentleman had missed and it arrived at Aylesbury first!

Perhaps it was only natural that signalmen and traffic controllers should give subconscious priority to their own companies trains, but it was the cause of increasing friction between them as the MS&LR expresses had to interweave between the Met commuter and freight trains over the Chiltern switchbacks.

The speed and vagueness of timing of the GCR trains over the Joint lines also led to conflict. This was exacerbated by the Daily Mail of July 1904 where an article criticised the poor speeds of British railways in comparison with their continental brethren, noting that the only exception was the smart running by the GCR on their Leicester–Marylebone expresses. These covered the 103 miles in 105 mins with an average speed of 58.8 mph, *"except they are much slower over the Quainton Road to London part due to the bad curves and steep gradients of the Metropolitan track"*. The Met Board saw this and Palmer (Superintendent of the Line) briefed them that the GCR trains were booked at 54 mph over his tracks but frequently exceeded this. Also in practice they often entered late and, as intermediate timings were not provided, one of their trains could hold up another. The GCR responded by saying that no other company required such timings and that their drivers always observed the cautions given to them by the Met. Palmer responded by again complaining about their speeding drivers, having just received a report of a GCR express being timed between Wendover and Aylesbury at 75 mph! In 1903 water troughs to the GWR design were installed at Charwelton, near Woodford, and then non stop running was possible over the 164¾ m from Marylebone to Sheffield at a scheduled time of 190 min, or an average speed of 52¼ mph.

Matters came to a head on the 23rd December 1904 when the 2.45am express parcels train from Marylebone reached Aylesbury station at 3.38am. The engine no.1040 with 10 coaches became derailed, mounted the platform and was completely wrecked. The fireman and another driver and fireman who were travelling as passengers in the first coach were killed instantly, whilst the driver was badly scalded and died of his injuries the next day. The other train-staff were badly shaken but fortunately the train was otherwise empty. However, immediately afterwards the GCR 10.20pm train from Manchester came into collision with the wreck, but it was travelling at a reduced speed which ensured that no further lives were lost. The subsequent inquiry was told that the visibility at that time was 20 yards but the fogmen and the signalmen had taken the appropriate precautions. Nevertheless Driver Bradshaw, who may have been unsure of the route, had been driving at excessive speeds earlier and significantly exceeded the 15mph speed limit at the approach to Aylesbury South. It was clear that a contributory factor was the severe reverse curve where the Met entered the station and it was recommended that this track layout should be changed.

Against this background of the continued operational problems and other unresolved issues such as the sharing of receipts, common fare structures and compensation for the Met, it all created a pressure to finalise a revision to the original 1890 Agreement between the parties for running the Extension. With Fay seeking resolution and on the other side, Lord Aberconway realising that the Met was losing its negotiating position as more GCR traffic could now go on to the GW & GC Joint line, the omens were right for a settlement. A new Heads of Agreement between the Met and GCR were signed on the 4th August 1905 and in essence stated that:

1) The additional parallel Met lines from Canfield Place to Harrow South Junction to be leased to the GCR for 999 years for £20,000 pa, with the Met having running powers from Neasden and Harrow South.
2) The Met Extension including the Chesham branch, but excluding the Uxbridge branch, to be leased to a Met & GCR Joint Committee at £44,000 pa for 999 years, each company to take turns for 5 years (beginning with the Met) to manage the line – or as agreed. Each company to use its own rolling stock.
3) The GCR not to convey local traffic to and from any point between Marylebone and Harrow South.
4) The Joint Committee to take over the responsibility of the Met in respect of the Brill Tramway. Willesden Green Station to be enlarged as an interchange station. The Met retaining its crossing to the south of the line at Wembley Park.
5) The GCR to guarantee traffic over the Joint Line at £45,000 pa gross.
6) Both companies allowed 33 1/3% of mileage receipts for running expenses of its own trains. The Joint Committee to pay all maintenance and other charges.
7) If in any year the Met mileage proportion of passenger traffic receipts between Baker Street and Harrow South Junction (relating to journeys between the Inner Circle and Harrow) fall below the estimated receipts for 1904 (because of the diversion of such traffic via Marylebone), then the GCR will pay the Met 66 2/3% of the mileage receipts between Marylebone and Harrow South in respect of such diverted traffic, up to the value of such ascertained receipts. Should this traffic exceed the 1904 figures, the balance (after deducting running expenses of 33 1/3% for each company) should be divided each half year: 3/5 to the Met and 2/5 to the GCR, and then in equal proportions. The GCR carryings to & from Marylebone for 1904 to be excluded from this.
8) Fares from Marylebone to Harrow and beyond not less than from Baker Street.
9) Further capital requirements for the Joint Line to be funded equally by both companies.

These came into operation on the 2nd April 1906, thus creating the Met & GC Joint Committee and at the same time the GCR took sole use of the two extra tracks built by the Met from Canfield Place to Harrow South Junction with the Joint. The Met could now hope to retain a reasonable proportion of the GCR mainline traffic that from the same date also had the option of using the new and easier GW & GC Joint line to the north. The GCR also benefited as their trains could now call at the Met stations from Harrow to Chesham and Quainton Road.

ooooO0Ooooo

Soon the basic problem of the Joint became apparent with the difficulty of scheduling the fast GCR expresses between the Met local trains. Matters came to a head in 1904 when a fast GCR mail train crashed at Aylesbury due to taking this south junction with the GWR, which was restricted to 15mph, at excessive speed. *(Clive Foxell Collection)*

The Marylebone early morning newspaper train took the 'S' bend at about 60mph, derailed and hit Aylesbury station killing four GCR crew aboard an otherwise empty train. Although the signalman acted quickly, an up train (hauled by another Robinson 11B) was unable to brake sufficiently to stop hitting the wreckage. (R Sedgewick Coll.)

The reason for the driver of the first train taking the junction at speed is unclear. Opinions differ on his knowledge of the 'road' and local witnesses testified to the dense fog at the time. It took several days to clear the track - it was littered with a batch of Xmas puddings! The damaged Robinson 11B lies in Aylesbury shed.*(R Sedgewick Coll)*

As a consequence of the ongoing disagreements between the Joint and the GWR as to who should have to pay for improving this dangerous junction it was not modified until 1907. Looking south from Aylesbury station, the work on slewing the track is in progress and the new south signal box has been completed. *(Colin Seabright)*

The new Robinson express locomotives were now in the ascendancy. He explored both 4-4-2 and 4-6-0 wheel arrangements and above one of his class 8B Atlantic's, no.1085 only one year old, nears Northwood on the first year of the Joint in 1906. *(Clive Foxell Collection)*

Robinson also introduced some 4-4-2 tank engines to deal with the growing commuter traffic over their lines to the west of London. The class 9L version seen above near Pinner in 1907, were deployed over the Joint , whilst the longer-range 9K's operated on the GW&GC services from Marylebone. *(Clive Foxell Collection)*

But soon the GCR needed larger engines to handle the popular local services over the Joint. The more powerful Robinson class 9N 4-6-2 tanks - known as GCrabs - were built for his purpose and served faithfully until almost the end of steam. This shows the new no.105 on the 3.20pm ex-Marylebone train at Pinner in 1911. *(Ken Nunn Coll./LCGB)*

A Met down train of around 1908 at Great Missenden station. It is headed by an F class 0-6-2 tank locomotive built around 1901 and consists of a horse box van, a milk van and a set of 4-wheel coaches. *(Colin Seabright)*

The first station built by the Joint was Waddesdon Manor in 1907, some 4 miles to the north of Aylesbury, to serve the Rothschild estate more conveniently than Waddesdon on the Brill branch. Interestingly the buildings were uniquely on the 'down' side. A Robinson Atlantic class 8B no.264 thunders past with an up express. *(Lens of Sutton)*

Aylesbury Joint (ie Met&GC and GC&GW) station after the realignment of the south junction in 1907, which is in the background. A GCR class 9L 4-4-2 local arrives at the down platform, whilst a rake of GWR clerestory coaches are in a siding on the right in front of the spartan 'shared' engine shed. *(Colin Seabright)*

Work had continued on improving the approaches to Harrow station to accommodate the GCR trains and the electrification of the Met lines to Harrow and Uxbridge. The new Met tracks are being built in the foreground, whilst a Pollitt class 11A 4-4-0 no.865 has passed under Sheepcote Road on the way to Marylebone. *(David Jackson Collection)*

By 1910 the Joint was settling down to a routine and allotments were springing up beside the line. Here a GCR Robinson class 8B Atlantic no.1089 heads a down express past Northwood to Manchester. *(GCRS)*

The Joint station at Rickmansworth around 1910. Staff are posed on the notoriously curved up platform, against the background of a fine array of Met station furniture. Rickmansworth staff had soon acquired the taste for traditional 'GCR tea', which was made by adding new tea leaves to those already in the pot! *(Clive Foxell Collection)*

The GCR locomotives that worked the Aylesbury - Verney Junction shuttle sometimes penetrated further into the Joint, apart from visits to their shed at Neasden. An example is this Sacré class 12AM 2-4-0T no.449 which simmers with a single van in the Chesham bay at Chalfont Road Station around 1910. *(R. Sedgewick Collection)*

The Joint re-laid the decrepit track of the Brill branch in 1910 and the maximum speed could be raised to 25mph! They also slightly improved the primitive stations and here at Westcott a sleeper-built platform has been added. Now, the once proud Met A class tanks were relegated to work the line with an Oldbury coach. *(Clive Foxell Collection)*

Electrification had reached Harrow in 1905, but a changeover to steam haulage had to be made for Met trains to continue over the Joint. Here in 1915 two Westinghouse camel-back Bo-Bo electric locos no.1&9 wait to return trains to the City, whilst a Met E class engine 0-4-4T no.79 is by the coaling stage near Sheepcote Rd. *(Ken Nunn/LCGB)*

CHAPTER 6

FORMING THE JOINT COMMITTEE

In the year between signing the Heads of Agreement and the start of the new regime in 1906 there was detailed work and long negotiations on exactly how it was to be implemented. Perhaps the obvious approach would have been to create an integrated company with single management of the finances, operations and assets. However with the long background of bickering and distrust between the two companies it was probably inevitable that each would wish to hang on to its own and also have complete visibility of the other party's activities. So complex working arrangements were agreed in which, under the Joint Committee, the control of the twin functions of management and accounts were rotated between the Met and the GCR on a five-yearly basis. The implementation of this compact was inevitably modified as time went by due to changes in ownership and wars, so the actual outcome of responsibility is shown below:

CHRONOLOGY OF RESPONSIBILITIES FOR THE JOINT

DATES	MANAGEMENT	ACCOUNTS
2-04-06 to 2-04-11	Met	GCR
3-04-11 to 2-04-16	GCR	Met
3-04-16 to 2-04-22	Met	GCR
3-04-22 to 2-04-26	GCR, then LNER	Met
3-04-26 to 31-12-31	Met	LNER
1-01-32 to 31-12-36	Met, then LT from 1-7-33	LNER
1-01-37 to 31-12-41	LT	LNER
1-01-42 to 31-12-46	LT	LNER
1-01-47 to 31-12-51*	LT	LNER
1-01-48 to 20-07-96	BR & LT	
21-07-96 to date	Railtrack, LT & Chiltern Rlys.	
* pre-war proposal		

The Joint Committee itself now employed all the staff to operate their line from Harrow South Junction to Quainton Road and Verney Junction, as well as the branches to Chesham and Brill. (the responsibilities for the latter branch having been assumed by the Joint). These staff included the signalmen, stationmasters &

men, goods yard & deliverymen etc.: but not the trains and their crews who remained with their own operating companies. Although the Joint Committee now owned their track, buildings and related assets, Watkin's Met had acquired a considerable amount of surplus lands and under the Agreement they retained these.

Under the 'management' and 'accounts' functions, at any given time one role was performed by the Met and the other by the GCR, alternating every 5 years. These responsibilities were defined as follows:

MANAGEMENT

Claims & refunds
Timetabling
Harrow Yard shunting engine
Goods, pw & signal staff, plus buildings
Manning of Harrow South signal box
Track maintenance (subsequently
   modified so that the Met was
   responsible for south of milepost 28½
   and the GCR north of it)

ACCOUNTS

Purchasing & supplies:
   i.e. clothing, stationery
Traffic returns
Timetable production
Joint excursion trains
Joint Cttee. Secretariat

These two functions were to be rotated between the two companies, but in addition a number of responsibilities were shared or dealt with by the company involved as follows:-

Lost property: That found on Met trains was to be returned to the Lost Property Office at Baker Street while that on GCR trains to the Office at Marylebone. However any found on Joint property and not claimed to be sold and the proceeds divided between the companies. (!)

Accidents: To be reported to both companies.

Breakdowns: To be dealt with by the relevant operating company.

Goods Trains serving the Joint to be worked on alternate weeks by each company. This rapidly proved unworkable and reverted to solely the Met.

Routing of goods traffic: Unassigned goods (i.e. those not marked by the sender to be consigned by either the Met or the GCR) to be sent by alternate companies each month (i.e. Jan 1932 via the LNER and Feb 1932 by the Met). Chesham station to be excluded from this arrangement. (!)

Although this convoluted structure was intended to ensure that neither company had the opportunity to manipulate the operation of the Joint to its own advantage, it was complex to work with the added prospects of an 'all-change' every five years to look forward to. At this time the supplies of everything from buttons to boots would change, as would many facets of day-to-day operations. It was also inefficient for each company to maintain groups of specialised staff that were only needed for five years out of ten. This consideration also applied to equipment where on the same basis, for example, the Met had for 5yr periods to provide shunting locomotives at Harrow Goods Yard for which it had little other use. Indeed these elaborate schemes probably only worked because the staff that had to operate it owed their primary allegiance to their employer, the Joint. Their station masters were the key factor in the day-to-running of the line and they adopted a pragmatic interpretation to the niceties of the rules in order to ensure that their customers (who most knew personally) got a good service.

Even so these station masters could only pity their colleagues at Aylesbury Joint station, which since 1906 had been shared by two joint companies (the Met & GC Joint and the GW & GC Joint Committees). Again the principle of 'alternation' was applied to the running of the station from 1907 and the practical complexity of this is shown below:

RESPONSIBILITIES FOR AYLESBURY STATION

DATES	CONTROL	MANAGEMENT	ACCOUNTS
1-08-21 to 31-03-27	GW & GC Jt.	GWR	Met
1-04-27 to 31-12-31	Met & GC Jt.	Met	GWR
1-01-32 to 31-12-36	GW & GC Jt.	GWR	LNER
1-01-37 to 31-12-41	Met & GC Jt.	LNER	Met
1-01-42 to 31-12-47	GW & GC Jt.	LNER*	GWR
1-01-48 to 20-07-96	BR & LT		

* requested by GWR

The prime authority of the Joint was defined in the Agreement as the 'Joint Committee' consisting of a Chairman and four representatives from each of the Met and the GCR. These were usually members of the respective Boards of the companies, although Officers could be invited to attend in a non-voting capacity. In addition, reporting to this body was an 'Officers Conference' with the same constitution, but of operational managers of both companies, that considered more mundane matters. The basic principal of the organisation of the Joint, namely 'alternation' was applied here as well. Meetings were normally held four times a year and the Chairman was alternated at each meeting as did the location so that a meeting at Baker Street would have a GCR Chairman and be followed next time at Marylebone with a Met Chairman. The Secretaries of the meetings came from the company having the 5 year responsibility for the accounts.

In spite of this formal committee structure most of the important work depended on tolerable personal relationships between the key players from both companies. For the smooth running of the Joint it was essential that the two people who managed the respective operations were able to work together. Although H B Palmer (Met Superintendent of the Line) and R Haigh Brown (GCR Superintendent) had previously fought for their own companies over details, they were able to 'bury the hatchet' - but they certainly marked the spot! For any concession they expected a similar one from the other company. Their Managing Directors, Fay and Ellis (and soon Selbie) were able to distance themselves from the arguments of the past and saw that both could share in any success of the 'Joint'. However both were particularly concerned with the financial consequences of the application of the Agreement and the commercial ramifications. Indeed both were assiduous observers at the Joint Committee meetings.

In some ways in the ongoing relationship, the Met saw itself as a patronised junior partner in relation to the grander GCR. This led to something of an inferiority complex which possibly fired their aspirations towards the status of a mainline railway.

ooooOOOoooo

The original formal seal which was created in 1906, but later wore out and had to be replaced in 1939.

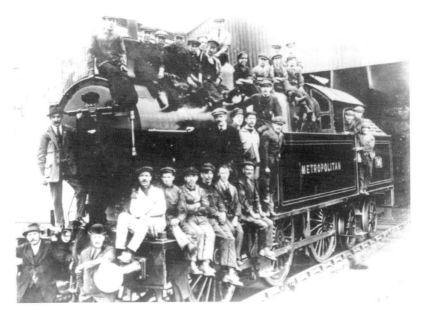

The Met G class 0-6-4T engines were introduced during the First War to cope with the new heavier Dreadnought coaches that had been built to equal the comfortable GCR coaches. The G class were also sometimes used for goods work and this photo shows the first of the class, no.94, at Neasden (Met) with most of the shed staff. *(CAF Coll)*

In 1909 Selbie signed an agreement with Denziel Davies of the Pullman Car Co. for them to provide two Pullmans for use between the City and Chesham, Aylesbury (seen here) & Verney Junction. Their buffer/coupling gear gave problems and the service ran at a loss, but they were retained for prestige until the war in 1939. *(H C Casserley)*

With the launch of MetroLand in 1915 there was a need for locomotives to haul the longer distance commuter trains and the Met introduced their H class 4-4-4T engines in 1920. Handsome and 'fleet of foot', they could also cope with sharp curves. Here one leaves Harrow with down train of a mix of Dreadnought and old bogie coaches. *(LT)*

These new Met locomotives allowed some of the earlier E class 0-4-4T's to be transferred to replace the original A class tank engines used on the Chesham shuttle. Here at Chesham station in the late 1920's the station master poses with the proud driver and guard beside the shuttle - now with Dreadnought coaches . *(Colin Seabright)*

Around 1930 a down Met train headed by an E class tank is about to pass a GCR Director with an express bound for Marylebone. Some E class tanks continued to haul Extension trains for many years until they were relegated to occasional standby duty at Rickmansworth - when they still performed well when needed. *(Patrick O'Hind)*

To reduce congestion on the Extension, the Joint increased the siding accommodation to allow longer goods trains. These needed more powerful engines and in 1925 the massive Met K class 2-6-4T's were delivered. The photo shows one on a down pickup goods at Quainton Road, whilst an A class no.23 waits with the Brill train. *(S H Freese)*

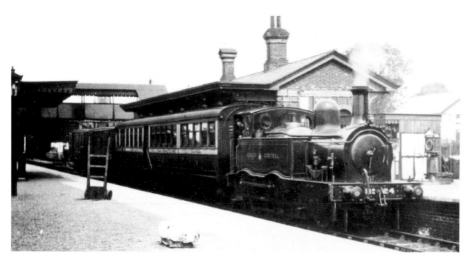

On the formation of the Joint the GCR offered to provide the Aylesbury-Verney Junction shuttle service. This operated six times/day in each direction and consisted of a Sacré class 12AM 2-4-0T no.24 and a GCR 12-wheeled railmotor coach, seen here at Aylesbury station around 1910 with 2 vans at the rear. *(Lens of Sutton)*

In the 1920's the Sacré tank engine that operated the Verney Junction shuttle was replaced by LNER with an ex-GER Holden 2-4-2 tank engine no.8307, which performed this duty until closure of Verney Junction to passengers in 1936. The picture shows the engine at Verney Junction around 1930. *(Richard Hardy)*

CHAPTER 7

THE CLASSIC YEARS

The period under the Joint Committee of 1906-1947 represents the high point of this story and extracts from the formal minutes of the Joint Committees in Appendix 1 illuminate the background. It brought together two quite different railways and cultures for it was said by a cynic that, *"the GCR was a northern freight railway with a branch to London, whilst the Met was an underground railway with pretensions to be a mainline"*.

In some ways the respective leaders of the GCR and the Met, Fay and Selbie, were similar people – being mature managers who had worked their way up their profession and who relished improving the performance of their companies. However it was inevitable that Fay in running a larger railway should take a broader view and concentrate on increasing the revenue to reduce their debt. In this context the Joint was a factor, but not a dominant one. Certainly exploiting the London commuter belt was important, but in many ways the less-well developed hinterland of the GW&GC Joint line offered him better prospects. By contrast, all Selbie had were the Circle, Hammersmith & East London lines apart from the Extension, most of which he shared with the GCR. These already carried substantial traffic and his prime concern was to increase this to pay for investment in extra capacity. Against this background Selbie took much greater interest in the details of operation and delegated less to his subordinates. For example, Fay could rest assured that Robinson at Gorton would develop and provide a range of competitive locomotive power to match the escalating GCR operating requirements, whereas it was Selbie who drove the much smaller Met engine programme through Jones and then Halley at the relatively basic works at Neasden. Selbie's attention to costs is also shown by his influence on Neasden where he closely monitored repair bills, time out of service and outside tenders. But he had the knack of striking the right balance and whilst the locomotives were largely built by contractors, they were suited to the Met, performed well and looked attractive. In all respects Selbie 'ran a tight ship' and kept his eyes open as he toured the system, constantly sending off a stream of memos to unfortunates who were slipshod or imprudent with the company's money. Amongst the employees the Met was known as the "*skilled with* **Scrap and** *know lady* **Luck**".

With the basic pattern of services well established before the formation of the Joint in 1906, Fay really only became concerned when there were any changes in these operations that might affect the financial interpretation of the Agreement. Thus the main disputes between the Met and the GCR (and their respective successors: LT and LNER) arose over two issues. Firstly, in general, Selbie was pushing for them both to invest in the infrastructure of the Joint in order to increase capacity i.e. rebuilding Aylesbury and Harrow stations, a branch to Watford, electrification etc., but Fay felt that the consequent benefits would mainly accrue to the Met. Secondly, when new operating arrangements were introduced by the Met or the GCR outside the remit of the Joint there could be a real or imagined impact on the traffic on the Joint itself, thus affecting the other partner. Obviously they only protested when this effect could be argued to be negative, as when the LNER the building of a loop line and station at Wembley in 1922, specifically to serve the new Exhibition and football stadium in competition with the Met: or when on the other side the Met proposed building a relief line in a tunnel from Kilburn to Edgware Road to ease the bottleneck between Finchley Road and Baker Street that might bypass the LNER. In addition there was a dispute which rumbled on over the attribution of revenue for tickets bought for travel to & from London, where the passenger could in practice use either company. Appendix 2 has a survey of the saga of the ongoing disputes over the interpretation of the Agreement.

As soon as the GW&GC Jt. Line was available Fay switched 4 of his Marylebone expresses to this slightly longer but better engineered route. These early GCR expresses were of impressive appearance with the smart Parker and Pollitt engines making a good turn of speed with the 4 or 5 corridor coaches (including at least a buffet car), which were more than adequate for the number of passengers at that time. To drum up business Fay launched a marketing campaign to attract passengers with their luxurious trains, weekend excursions and via collaboration with other railways, a host of destinations. The GCR gave the impression that it was possible – if not reasonable – to reach anywhere in Britain from Marylebone. As passenger numbers slowly increased and trains lengthened, the new Robinson engines began to take over. First were the class 8B Atlantics, with such graceful lines that they were called 'Jersey Lily's', after the King's mistress, and the 8C 4-6-0 version which were good performers with the 167 miles to Sheffield being covered in 170 min. As the GCR semi-fast trains called at Harrow and Aylesbury they competed directly with the Met and this was increased in 1907 when slip coaches were added to some trains. For example the 1.40pm down express slipped a coach at Amersham at 2.13pm which then called at Great Missenden at 2.24pm. The GCR local trains were the province of Robinson's new 4-4-2 tank engines: the Class 9K working the Joint and the similar longer range 9L type the GW&GC line. It took until 1907 for the partners to agree the precise interpretation of item 7 in the 1905 Agreement relating to the diversion of traffic from the Joint by such GCR train services to Aylesbury via High Wycombe.

Nevertheless, as a whole freight traffic tended to dominate the GCR, drawing on its original hinterland in the North Midlands where investment was made into port and wagon handling facilities at Immingham, Wath and later, Grimsby. But most of the movements to the south used the GW&GC Jt line rather than the Joint.

By the time Selbie took full control of the Met in 1908 his plans were well developed. Being an enthusiast for the electrification to Harrow & Uxbridge, it was obvious that as traffic on the Joint grew it would be a candidate for further electrification beyond Harrow. To obtain this expansion in passengers he built upon the existing trend for people to commute from Bucks, Herts and Middlesex to work in London. In this he was indebted to Watkin for negotiating for the Met the right to retain land surplus to building the Extension. Selbie saw that this land could be exploited for the creation of large housing estates of a quality that would attract the relatively affluent who could afford to commute in exchange for living in a pleasant environment. His concept of providing what would now be known as an integrated housing and transport system in an arcadian setting would benefit the Met during the initial building phase and then secure the ongoing visitor and season ticket revenues. He brought this together in 1915 under the banner of the MetroLand publicity campaign which struck a chord with generations of home seekers.

This needed trains with greater capacity matched by improved stations and facilities. Passenger trains were required of better quality in order to match the superior GCR local trains with which the Met was now in competition on the Joint. Higher acceleration was needed in order to increase train frequency but a limiting factor was also the number of ever longer goods trains occupying the line whilst shunting, due to the limited siding capacity. To this end during his office more powerful passenger and freight locos were introduced, first were the G Class 0-6-4T goods engines planned in 1910 to replace the old F Class, but delayed due to the war until 1915/6. Built by the Yorkshire Engine Company they had difficulty negotiating sharp curves, i.e. Chesham branch, and to Selbie's annoyance were often out of action with cracked frames. The complementary passenger H Class 4-4-4T's were more successful. Supplied by Kerr Stuart to a basic Neasden outline drawing and interestingly incorporating some GCR features, they were delivered in 1920/1 and came to dominate the passenger services beyond Rickmansworth. To match the luxurious GCR coaches the Met introduced in 1912/3 some comparable new coaching stock of such stolid appearance that they were called 'Dreadnoughts', but even so the H Class locos could haul them at speeds in excess of 75mph. However the pride of the Met fleet were the massive K Class 2-6-4T engines which were assembled by Armstrong Whitworth from modified war surplus components that had been made in Woolwich Arsenal originally to an SECR N Class design of Maunsell. These were tall and large engines and on a first outing on the Joint one took almost an inch off the edge of Moor Park platform. Nevertheless their power now enabled longer freight trains to be handled and which, in conjunction with a rolling programme of extending sidings from Willesden to Quainton Road, reduced the blocking of the growing passenger services.

For the electrification to Harrow and Uxbridge the local service was provided firstly by converting the 1889 Ashbury steam-hauled coach sets to BTH electric traction and then by ordering over 1905-7 6-car sets of multiple electric stock from Metropolitan Amalgamated with BTH/Westinghouse power units. Longer distance Met trains over the Joint were now brought to Harrow by new electric locos from BTH and Westinghouse for which facilities for changing to steam power for the onward journey had to be provided together with water, coaling and stabling sidings. Work had started on enlarging Harrow from 2 to 4 platforms to cope with the extra Uxbridge branch traffic in 1907. There was a hold-up due to the need to consider a proposal from a Mr Bliss who wanted the Met to use some of his land to make the main entrance to the station in Station Road on the east, but this was rejected in favour of an entrance on the west side. Track was doubled from Harrow South Junction, where a new frame of 32 levers was installed, through the station where the former up platform was converted into an island and a new up platform built to the east – all connected by bridge and subway. Harrow station box had a new frame of 70 levers and the north box at the Uxbridge junction some 50 levers. All was approved by Major Pringle of the Inspectorate on the 29th July 1908 and then the complaints from the GCR started on the 16th September! The nub of these was the objection that many of the improvements served the Met , rather than the Joint, and thus the GCR could not pay for them. These included the coal stage, engine pits, water columns, certain paths, the new Station Road bridge, lighting, and the extension of a shunting 'neck' near Roxborough bridge. Correspondence flowed at lower levels for years before petering out, but a question of who should man the Harrow South Junction signal box had to be referred to the Joint Committee to decide that it should be a Joint box with 5yr alternating responsibility.

The next station under the aegis of the Joint was proposed by a syndicate building a golf course at Sandy Lodge on the estate of Lord Ebury and the Committee agreed, provided the promoters guaranteed a revenue of more than £350 pa. In 1910 the construction of a halt was approved at a cost of £555 using old sleepers and without the provision of water or toilets. The subsequent offer by Lord Ebury to sell some of his land for sidings was not taken up until 1923 when it changed its name to Moor Park & Sandy Lodge to serve the development of the Estate. It later became a convenient interchange when the Watford branch was built. Further developments around 1910 revealed Selbie's intentions to upgrade the Met. These started with the largely symbolic gestures of the introduction of Pullman cars and in 1912 the laying of the foundation stone for the new headquarters building over Baker Street station which was to include offices, luxury flats, restaurant etc. These acts gave out the message that the Met was a railway to be reckoned with and strengthened his position in the rationalisation debates that he knew were inevitable. Selbie readily accepted the approach in 1908 by the Pullman Car Co. to encourage the use of their first class services by adding two of their luxurious coaches to prime trains on the Extension. 'Mayflower' & 'Galatea' (named after contending yachts for the America Cup) came into service in 1910: the agreement being that the Pullman Co. provided the coaches & attendants and received the supplement fares of 6d to Rickmansworth or 1/- beyond to Chesham & Verney Junction, whilst the Met hauled the coaches, kept 'the working parts' in good condition and received the normal fares. Soon there were practical problems interfacing their buffers & draw gear and, although modifications were made to adjacent Met stock, there was still a tendency for buffers to lock on sharp curves. Whilst Selbie retained them for prestige, in themselves they never made a profit. Typically around the 1912/5 period some 12,000 passengers were carried in the year, few using them between the City and Harrow and the majority beyond, giving a loss of about £1,300 pa – a share of which had to be absorbed by the Joint. Various attempts were made to increase patronage by better advertising, reducing the supplement to a flat 6d and lunch from 4/6 to 3/6 but it remained a flagship service until withdrawn on the 7th October 1939 after the outbreak of the war.

However more pragmatic were the improvements over 1911/2 to improve the capacity between Baker Street and Harrow. A combination of automatic signalling from the City to Neasden which enabled much closer running of trains and the construction of two extra tracks from Finchley Road to Wembley Park giving further capacity soon enabled the passenger-miles to be doubled since the turn of the century.

The success of his electrification policy confirmed Selbie's view of the benefits of extending it along the Joint line and the trigger came from the pressure from the people of Watford who had lobbied the Met since the 1880's for a branch to their town, being unhappy with the service provided by the LNWR. As a result of a local council petition in 1906 the question of building a branch was formally considered by the Joint and, as might be expected, the GCR were reluctant to participate as they believed that the Met would again be the main beneficiary. Nevertheless it was agreed to undertake a survey of the possible route and this was tabled later at a Joint meeting in 1911, where due note was taken of the possibility of extending such a branch to the north to St. Albans to ward off the competition from the electrification schemes of the LNWR. Much was also made of the freight prospects of the paper industry growing around Watford. The GCR agreed to support the branch as they wished to run trains to Marylebone but the enabling Bill was to be progressed by the Met, with powers vested in the Joint. There was violent criticism from the LNWR, who only succeeded in forcing the Met to raise the height of their line so that the LNWR Croxley branch could be extended underneath, but the more surprising and damaging opposition came from Watford Council to the location of the Met terminus in the High Street – causing them to inconveniently re-site it near Cassiobury Park. The Royal Assent was given to the Bill in 1912 and a Watford Joint Railway Committee was established to fund the work in which electrification was implicit, starting by acquiring the necessary lands. No sooner had substantial land been purchased from Gonville &

Caius College in 1914 than the First War started and, whilst land purchases in progress were completed, construction was suspended.

Selbie might have realised that war was inevitable because he rejected Fay's reasonable proposal that, in view of the light traffic, the Joint should 'single' the double track from Quainton Road to Verney Junction thus saving £565 pa. It could have been an attachment to this outpost of the Met with its memories of Messrs Watkin, Verney and Buckingham (for he resisted this move while he was in charge), but more likely he foresaw that within a few months this line would became a vital link in the war effort. From the start of the war the 130 UK railways were placed under the control of the Railway Executive Committee in order to co-ordinate their activities in relation to the priorities of the war effort. This recognised what was already apparent: namely fragmentation was hindering service, efficiency and progress. The financially vulnerable GCR had been seeking consolidation with the GNR and GER, whilst the Met recognised the ambitions of London Underground. So the creation of the REC highlighted the problem but this forestalled any action. The GCR and Met tried to cope with 30% extra passengers, troop & ambulance trains and in transporting vast amounts of coal for the war effort from the collieries served by the GCR The magnitude is indicated by the fact that the Navy was entirely fuelled by coal and just for them the GCR ran some 1930 trains to move it to the ports. All this had to be done with a reduction in coal supply of 20%, loss of staff to the forces and some Zeppelin bombing. Women were employed extensively for the first time as cleaners, guards and in the signal boxes. Services were restricted to some extent, for example the Met favoured longer distance travellers by moving the changeover to steam haulage back to Wembley Park and some trains continued to do so until 1919. Goods traffic saturated Verney Junction and troop movements to Wendover, for Halton Camp, increased by 250% over peace time, but overall the GCR & Met performed better than most during the war.

At the outbreak of war a military camp had been established in the grounds of the de Rothschild estate at Halton and with the arrival of the RFC soon grew to some 20,000 men, many of whom used the nearby Wendover station. The Joint station master, Thomas Read, noted the vast supplies being brought to the camp by road and proposed (complete with plans) to the Met Board, that a light railway line be built from no.1 siding at his station to the camp. He received £250 for his initiative and the 1¾ m line was built by German POW's, opening under military auspices in 1917. To access the nearby trees for supplies of wood, a 2ft narrow gauge extension was built across the Icknield Way. Initially a Met loco was used on the standard gauge section, but in 1919 the Camp obtained two 0-6-0T engines of their own from Scotland. To complete the story, the Camp continued in use after the war, albeit on a reduced scale, only to expand again with the second world war, by when the haulage was by two Fowler 0-6-0 diesel locos. After the war the demand for coal by the site declined and the Halton Light Railway closed on 31st March 1963.

At the north end of Rickmansworth some 10 years after electrification. The Met Bo-Bo electric no.14 'Benjamin Disraeli' has come off the incoming train to Aylesbury and is passing by to pick up the next up train to London. Meanwhile the Met H class no.106 waits to back onto the down train. All this in less than 3 minutes! *(H C Casserley)*

Although the new Met multiple electric T stock for the Watford & Rickmansworth services had been delivered in 1926, the older units remained in use for several years. Here such a set of the 1905 Met-Cammell stock form a slack hour Watford-Aldgate train, near Northwood in 1937. *(John Parnham)*

The Watford branch had been mooted since 1906 but it was not completed until 1925. The line was opened on the 25th of October by this special train from Baker Street, seen passing Croxley Green, with the Lords Faringdon and Aberconway travelling in the Met Directors saloon - formerly belonging to the Rothschilds.

The Watford branch was the responsibility of a new joint Met & LNER committee which reported to the Joint. It opened with a remarkable service of 40 Met & 30 LNER trains/day, but the General Strike in 1926 gave the LNER the excuse to cancel their trains. Note the characteristic Met 'diamond' logo for the station name. *(Lens of Sutton)*

Accelerating rapidly round the curve from Aylesbury Joint station, past the north signal box, is a double-headed down express in 1934. The leading engine is an ex-GCR class 8B no.5263, which is piloting no.5433 an ex-GCR class D10 4-4-0 Director. *(GCRS)*

A photo of Aylesbury station in 1936 which epitomises the second phase of the Joint. Although the owners have changed the atmosphere remains much the same. The LNER no.6091 ex-GCR class 8B still looks magnificent, whilst the LT train in the bay, also for London, is headed by an ex-Met liveried class H no.104. *(H C Casserley)*

Another ex-GCR 'Jersey Lilly', LNER no.5262, accelerates in a resounding manner out of the sharp curve through Rickmansworth station on the 08.57 down train to Leicester in 1938. This and a number of the other photographs were taken from the trackside by John Parnham, who was then a young surveyor working on the Joint line.

Poetry in motion! Now LNER, a B3/2 4-6-0 no.6166 'Earl Haig' whose name had such a powerful resonance for so many people in the pre-war years. Here at speed on an up ex-Woodford train near Watford Road signal box in 1937. *(John Parnham)*

A view from the footbridge to the south of Rickmansworth station looking towards the Met goods shed. An ex-Met H class no.103 is about to take the crossover on to the down road to join the next train to Aylesbury. Meanwhile two Bo-Bo electric locos nos. 3&8 wait for the next LT up trains. *(John Parnham)*

Another ex-GCR class 8B no.5266 on a London Excursion train in the early 1930's passing through Wendover station. The signal at the end of the up platform is backed by white boarding to give greater clarity. *(Colin Seabright)*

LNER no.5507 D11, an ex-GCR 11F improved Director class, named 'Gerard Powys Dewhurst' on a down milk train with empty tank wagons. The daily working was back via Woodford, Oxford GWR and to Dorrington milk depot in Shropshire. *(J Parnham)*

The early 1898 teak Ashbury coaching stock, later converted for multiple electric sets in 1906, continued in use on the Joint until put into a strategic reserve before the 1939 war. Here is such a set near Watford Road Junction and in the background can be seen the white sub-station with the junction signal box in front. *(John Parnham)*

An LNER class L1 2-6-4T (ex-GCR class 1B) no. 5340 leaves Rickmansworth past the LT loco coaling siding on the morning down goods train for the stiff climb up the Chilterns to Amersham. *(John Parnham)*

From 1936 the dominance of ex GCR Robinson locomotives on the expresses over the Joint began to be eroded by the new LNER Gresley class B17 'Sandringhams'. Here no. 2842 'Kilverstone Hall' is on the 15.20 down express form Marylebone. It is pounding past the flagman, one Fidler, beside a dumpy level made in the 1890's. *(John Parnham)*

Although the war ended in 1918 the railways remained under Government control as the effectiveness of the REC had demonstrated the need for rationalisation. It also benefited the Treasury as although they bore all costs and took all revenues they only paid the railways the 1913 profits, whereas in practice these were higher in the war due to the heavier traffic! By 1920 the Government produced a proposal to consolidate the 'London railways' but Selbie successfully argued that the Met was incompatible with the 'Underground Group' and was excluded from the subsequent Railways Act of 1921, which created the 'big four grouping' of 1923. The Met now had a good fleet of steam locos and also the Watford and electrification plans could resume.

The GCR had reached its zenith by way of a succession of locomotives produced by Robinson. His class 8F 'Immingham' 4-6-0's of 1906 were for express goods work, then the 8G mixed traffic types which were basically smaller coupled-wheel versions of the earlier 8C class, whilst he experimented with compounding in the following class 8D&E 4-4-2 engines. To sustain the heavier suburban schedules from Marylebone the class 9N 4-6-2T locos were introduced in 1911 and were to continue in these duties for 40 years. These were just one of his long-lived designs, some of which were perpetuated by the LNER and survived to serve in BR or, as with the classic class 8K 2-8-0 heavy freight engines, saw extensive service in two wars. Next in 1913 came the Robinson use of inside cylinders for express work with the class 1 'Sir Sam Fay' 4-6-0 locos and the smaller-wheeled mixed-traffic 'Glenalmond' class 1A, but the Joint will always be associated with the following class 11 E&F 'Director' express passenger engines. Also features of the later Joint line were the class 1B 2-6-4 tank engines, originally built in 1914 for the northern coal trade. But the culmination of Robinson's express designs was the large class 9P 4-6-0 built in 1917 which appropriately was named after their Chairman Lord Faringdon, and with the rest of the class constructed in 1920 became a feature of the crack Marylebone trains and were often seen on the heavy excursions over the Joint.

The original Joint Committee met for the last time on the 24th November 1922 when the main topic was the tendering for the re-commencement of the construction of the Watford branch. Sir Sam Fay objected to the inclusion of a 'north curve' at the junction between the branch and the Extension, as this would only benefit the Met, and it was excluded from the initial tenders. He retired from the Committee and the GCR at the end of the year. However it was obvious to Selbie that the war, REC and grouping had changed the prospects of an independent Met and soon the General strike in 1926 and bus competition would further reduce his options. So it was his aim to maximise the bargaining power of the Met for the inevitable negotiation on any amalgamation , but paradoxically the grouping of the GCR with its erstwhile collaborators into the massive LNER tended to enhance the Joint in the short term – which even retained its constitution and name as the Met & GC Joint Committee.

oooo000oooo

CHAPTER 8

CHANGE YOUR PARTNERS

In the new Joint Committee Haigh Brown, who had a long career with the MS&LR and the GCR, now represented the LNER. At his first meeting he inherited Fay's reluctance to bow to the pressure of Sir Harry Verney of the Met (and Aylesbury) to agree to rebuild Aylesbury station. Following the terrible accident here in 1904 the much criticised junction between the Met, GWR and ex-A&BR lines had been re-laid and the South signal box relocated. However this left the basic station in a relatively primitive condition, considering the increasing amount of traffic and importance of the prosperous county town, and so the inhabitants were understandably very unhappy over the lack of action. To get any decision from the tripartite owners (GWR, Met and GCR) was difficult, but the war had then delayed matters further and when a rebuilding scheme was drawn up in 1922 the cost of £36,000 was such that Fay could not see the benefit to the GCR – possibly influenced by their imminent merger into the LNER. It took a delegation from the town to Marylebone in 1923 to meet Selbie, Sir Ralph Wedgwood (GM LNER) and Sir Felix Pole (GM GWR) to get action and in 1924 the Joint agreed to spend £61,114 on a new station, of which the Met paid about 25%, plus performing significant work themselves. Designed by C J Brown of the LNER with an improved track layout the platforms were doubled in length and a new footbridge, goods shed, coal yard and offices, it opened in 1926.

However the associated engine shed remained fairly primitive and apart from being the only shed on the Joint (the nearest relevant ones being at Neasden and Woodford), it had the distinction of being shared between the partners in Aylesbury. But whereas the management of the station rotated amongst them, in the case of the engine shed the GWR, Met and GCR/LNER had separate enclaves. The GWR had 4 crews, 5 cleaners and a fitter who looked after 2 locos working the service to Princes Risborough, the Met had 4 crews and a fitter to run the class A , D &F engines, whilst the GCR based up to 4 locos there with 4 crews, 5 cleaners and a foreman. Facilities were rudimentary, lacking proper toilets and washing facilities for many years. Water for the engines was pumped from a stream by the engines themselves into a tank which was over a very basic coal stage.

When the Met had taken over the A&BR Aylesbury became the base for a shuttle service to Verney Junction. Initially this was provided by LNWR engines until the Met D class were delivered but with the creation of the Joint the GCR offered to operate this train. At first ex-MS&LR 2-4-0 outside framed Sacré tanks were used but with grouping LNER 2-4-2T's worked the service with an ex-GCR Parker class F1 and an ex-GER F7, which sometimes worked on to Risborough.

When work was ready to start again on the Watford branch in 1923, Selbie clearly saw it as part of his plan to electrify the Met from Harrow to Rickmansworth and eventually to Amersham. The LNER were uneasy over this as they felt that this would improve the Met's share of business over the Joint, but could only claim that if they acquired electric stock, then they would have the right to use the electrified tracks. On this basis the cost of the electrification scheme was split equally, although for the section through Harrow station which also carried the solely Met service to Uxbridge, they had to pay 55%. The LNER also complained that the additional Met service to Watford would cause congestion at Harrow North junction with the Uxbridge branch – ignoring the fact that the LNER also wished to operate a Watford service to Marylebone. Selbie countered with a proposal to build a burrowing junction at this point to ease the Uxbridge flow and when he offered to pay 75% of the £77,000 cost, the LNER agreed. The electrification, including power supplies and improved signalling, was completed to Rickmansworth by mid-1925 and the changeover from steam to electric traction was now performed here.

The completion of the new double-track 2m 37ch branch to Watford was delayed due to the difficult soil conditions encountered by Logan & Hemmingway at the junction with the main line. These problems were acknowledged by the Joint in releasing the contract 'retention' early and agreeing the extra costs involved. However there was disagreement within the Joint over the need for a north curve at the junction that would enable trains to run into Watford from Rickmansworth and the north, which the LNER saw as favouring the Met and thus a way of saving money. It took a joint letter from both of the General Managers to get agreement, but then the LNER insisted on simplifying the proposed signalling. The Met paid £3,325 for the new changeover facilities and bay for a Watford 'shuttle' at Rickmansworth. The branch was ceremonially opened by a special train from Baker Street on the 31st October 1925, which included Lord Aberconway (Met), Lord Faringdon (LNER) and distinguished guests travelling in the Directors' saloon, which had been converted from the original coach of Baron Ferdinand de Rothschild. They were met by the Mayor of Watford and dignitaries from Rickmansworth who had arrived by the new 'shuttle' train. After the formalities they all retired to the Oddfellows Hall for a traditional repast. The public service started on the 2nd November with the incredible number of 40 up & down Met trains giving a 35 min journey to Baker Street, plus 30 more LNER to & from Marylebone. The location of the station did not produce enough passengers to justify this service and with 670,000 travelling in the first year the loss ran at about £7,000, but goods traffic made a small profit of £670 and soon grew taking paper contracts from the LMS and with new business additional lorries (with Metro & LNERlys. signs) were needed. With the General Strike of

1926 the opportunity was taken by the LNER to cease their trains and with this lower cost base and the building of housing estates in the vicinity, results began to improve. A further boost was given by the popularity of the local football club which encouraged the running of specials to & from the other club's town. This was one of the few services that the Joint was allowed to advertise under its own banner and for a 'good London match' some 4-5,000 would travel to the game by these trains.

Football had an even greater impact via the creation of the British Empire Exhibition at Wembley, with the first building being the Football Stadium constructed on the site of the demolished Watkin Tower and opened for the Cup Final in 1923. The building of this and the adjacent Exhibition which was largely fabricated from concrete involved much material being transported over the Joint from Rickmansworth and elsewhere. These events justified an intensive service from London and many specials for both partners, but the inevitable competition and the decision by the LNER to open a loop station on the site led to much friction within the Joint. A significant Met exhibit in the Palace of Engineering was one of the 20 new 1,200 hp 61½ ton Bo-Bo electric locomotives from Metropolitan-Vickers which were designed for high acceleration from 20 sec stops on the underground section, covering the non-stop run to Harrow in 15 min and eventually a set of Dreadnought coaches up the Chilterns to Amersham. New multiple-electric compartment units from the same company, called 'MW' then later 'T' stock, had also been ordered for the extra Exhibition and Watford branch services. With these, and the H & K class locomotives for work beyond Rickmansworth, Selbie now had a very satisfactory fleet to operate over the Joint.

In the background from 1925–30 the disputes between the partners continued over the interpretation of the Agreement, centering on running powers, division of receipts, attribution of season ticket revenues and the general decline in LNER use of the Joint. Selbie argued with Wedgewood (Dep. Ch. LNER) that the Met were expending large sums to improve their Joint lines by electrification and also by widening the tracks from Finchley Road to Wembley Park, both of which attracted more traffic to the Joint from which the LNER would benefit *'although being a slothful partner'*. He became more concerned over this point in 1925 when the Met sought to ease the bottleneck caused by the tunnel between Finchley Road & Baker Street by driving another tunnel from Willesden Green to near Edgware Road on the Inner Circle line. Counsels' opinion was sought regarding the effect on revenue sharing on the Joint, and although as described in Appendix 2 this gave little comfort to the Met, in practice the tunnel never came to fruition due to cost and safety issues. However in anticipation, Edgware Road station was rebuilt to receive the tunnel with indicators that could display Verney Junction as a destination.

The growth of goods traffic exacerbated another Met concern relating to an earlier 'alternating' arrangement that they had agreed in 1906 whereby each company would work the goods trains on alternate weeks. This proved impractical and soon the Met took over all local haulage for a lower fee. However as freight increased the Met lost more money, rising to £9,777 in 1925 , due to these unrealistic charges plus inadequate wagon storage. By 1927 even the LNER had to agree that the fee should be increased and that they should contribute towards extra siding capacity. The Met K class locos could now handle 600 ton trains with ease but these were longer and sidings had been lost in other improvements, such as building the burrowing junction at Harrow. At this yard the goods tonnage had risen from 28,835 tons in 1921 to 62,697 in 1924 so that some goods trains had to be diverted to Willesden Green, because the sidings were full. As a result by 1927 a programme had been completed to add extra siding capacity at Harrow, Northwood, Rickmansworth, Amersham and Quainton Road which was now dealing with up to 2,500 LNER wagons a week.

This growth was due to the continued development of the northern GCR freight base by the LNER after grouping, although only a small part of this mainly mineral and fish business was routed over the Joint. On the passenger side the LNER timetable remained much the same, with the only real change being the inclusion in 1929 of an extra express at 4.55pm from Marylebone to Manchester. By contrast they did encourage the use of the Joint for the boom in excursion (including 'mystery trips'), overnight and other specials to add to the newspaper and mail trains. Probably due to inertia, the relevant operating departments remained in the hands of ex-GCR staff and Robinson engines continued to hold sway but by the 1930's a variety of LNER types began to appear. These included some Gresley A1 Pacific's, V2 2-6-2's, K3 2-6-0's, V1 2-6-2 tanks as possible replacements for the ex-GCR 9N class, and a larger number of B17 4-6-0 'Football's'.

1929 saw the passing of the Metropolitan Rly. Development Act which enabled work to start on a branch to Stanmore and, for the Joint, the significant completion of the 4 tracks to Harrow. The long-awaited HQ at Baker Street was now almost complete. However these turned out to be a final flourish for the Met for the new Labour Government, pushed by Herbert Morrison, revived the intention to amalgamate transport in London. Again Selbie led the fight to exclude the Met but tragically he died suddenly on 17th May 1930 whilst attending a confirmation service, which included his son, at St. Pauls's Cathedral. Having lost his key Director, Lord Aberconway the Met Chairman recognised that amalgamation was inevitable and it was now a question of obtaining the best terms. In this he was supported by their legal advisor John Anderson, who became temporary General Manager of the Met. They faced the formidable Lord Ashfield the potential head of the embryonic transport body for London. The Met tried various compromises that would leave them more or less intact but soon they were forced to seek the best financial deal they could for absorption. In this a Met director, Dudley Docker, acted as an intermediary with the new Government of 1931, in which a Liberal Minister Percy Pybus surprisingly reinforced the amalgamation policy of his Labour predecessor. The key elements in the settlement became: 1) the value of the Met, as the latest financial results were deteriorating 2) the value of the Met assets and in that they set aside replacement at original, rather than current cost, as did most other London railways 3) the value of LT stock for conversion of Met stock and guarantees for future dividends 4) confirmation of exclusion of Met. Rly. Country Estates. An Extraordinary Meeting of Met shareholders agreed to accept LT A&B shares in exchange for their preference shares at a conversion rate to give the same income, whilst ordinary shareholders could have either LT C stock at 67.1% or what turned out to be a better offer of a new share guaranteed to yield 3¼ % for 15yrs.

On the 1st July 1933 the LPTB came into being and took over responsibility for the Met participation in the Joint. Although the partners were now the LNER and LT it remained the Met & GC Jt. Committee but, significantly their first meeting on 23rd November was held at 55 Broadway with Lord Ashfield, Sir John Gilbert & Frank Pick for LT and Hon E Butler-Henderson & W B Gair of the LNER. Soon senior LNER directors, Sir Ralph Wedgwood & William Whitelaw, began to attend in view of the wider relationship with LT. The more that Pick saw of the Met , the less he liked it and in December he sent a memo to Anderson claiming that the maintenance standards of the Met had been too low and that the final accounts of the Met should have reflected this *"but a bargain was done and the matter is closed"*. This theme continued in the 1935 LT Annual Report : *"the principal efforts have been directed towards bringing the standards & practices of the former Met, which had been operated on lines more akin to those of a main line company, into conformity"*. By this time Anderson had been made Solicitor and his colleagues dispersed around LT so that they had little contact with the Met.

From 1936 Pick set about removing the 'anomalies' of the Met, of which steam operation was the main candidate. Following a brief flirtation with diesel power, in the form of the trial of a GWR/AEC railcar on the Chesham branch in March 1936, LT sought a way to extract themselves from responsibility for steam power and plan for further electrification of the Joint. An excuse was found when Neasden works came under the control of LT Acton works, who wanted to enlarge the existing multiple-electric stock sheds – which they claimed would leave no space for the Met engine shed and works. On this basis an agreement was reached with the LNER for them to take over (from 1st November 1937) the majority of the Met steam locos, base them at the their own shed at Neasden and provide freight services over the Joint. For this the LNER was paid 1/3 of the revenues plus 15/10 per engine hour and 2/- per guard hour. Whereas for hauling LT trains beyond Rickmansworth the rate was 25/- per engine hour. Met crew were loaned to the LNER, retaining their conditions & uniforms and with the option of transferring to electric stock – or 'the juice' as it was known! The capital charge to the LNER for the 18 Met Locos and various wagons was £39,050. In a similar manner the steam services beyond Aylesbury had come under close scrutiny before being passed to the LNER. The Brill branch was closed on 30th November 1935, Waddesdon station soon after and on the 4th July 1936 the line from Quainton Rd. to Verney Junction was singled with the loss of passenger services, but it remained open for goods traffic until 28th January 1940.

Some animosity lingered between the old Joint staff and their new LT colleagues. For a time at Harrow signalbox, some would not speak directly to the LT signalmen (who they referred to as 'boardsmen') and would only pass instructions via the boy in the box. Whilst many of the idiosyncrasies of the Met disappeared, the majority of travellers still continued to encounter the traditional Met experience, rather longer than LT expected. For by the time of the Czechoslovakian crisis in 1938 the prospect of another war came nearer and the Ministry of Transport again appointed an embryonic Railway Executive Committee to advise them on preparations that the railways should make for such an emergency. These included bringing the railway companies together into one organisation, war precautions, civil and military transport needs (including evacuation) and strategic supply routes. With the outbreak of war imminent, on the 1st September 1939 the REC took complete control and implemented their contingency plans. Part of these were a large number of schemes designed to speed up war traffic and provide relief routes avoiding those centres likely to suffer from severe bombing. In the later stages of the war these and new schemes were deployed to facilitate the heavy flow of traffic in connection with the invasion of the Continent. A main alternative route was needed to and from the Southern Railway system avoiding the London junctions and it was agreed that traffic from the LNER and LMS would be routed via Sandy, Bedford, Bletchley, Verney Junction, Calvert, Staines Moor, Merstham and Tonbridge. To provide this route several extra junctions were constructed, including Calvert with a double-line connection between the LNER(GC) and LMS lines finally opened in 1940. This was heavily used during and after the war and made the old Verney Junction to the Joint redundant.

War had quickly imposed numerous restrictions on the railways in terms of travel restrictions, blackout (including loco cabs and ash pits), a maximum speed of 50mph, withdrawal of Pullmans and similar luxuries and priority for the war effort. The first test of the planning of the REC was the mass evacuation of children from major towns in the south. The Joint carried large numbers in special trains to be billeted in the Chilterns and the Vale of Aylesbury, but the majority probably drifted back home over time. This area was also ideal for locating military units i.e. Coastal Command HQ at Northwood, US Army around Amersham, Halton returning to its former glory, and the Vache at Chalfont as a POW reception centre. These needed numerous troop trains which usually exceeded 12 coaches in length. New airfields were built at Bovingdon, Westcott and elsewhere, with an insatiable need for petrol supplies. Equally manufacturing companies moved out of London to avoid the heavy bombing or to act as satellite suppliers for war production and many, such as Shackmans in Chesham, stayed on after the war. A number of factories became of strategic importance like International Alloys at Aylesbury, a major supplier of aluminium fabrications for aircraft, and who were provided with their own siding. All these activities produced heavy and unpredictable traffic for the Joint, let alone the specials they were still expected to provide.

An example of the latter was on the 16th May 1942 when a special train was provided to return Molotov (the Russian Foreign Minister on his first visit to Britain) with Churchill from a secret meeting at Halton Camp by train from Wendover to Marylebone. Matt Robinson (Neasden Superintendent) wrote to Inspector Goodhand to inform him that loco A5 no.5003 would not now be used as the train could not stop for water and that it would be replaced by D11 no.5510. *"It should not be used for any other jobs prior to this special and be examined for sands, brake & injectors. In addition the Chargeman should endeavour to see that the motion is specially cleaned."* The loco was to run light & tender first to Verney Junction where it would pick up a special set of LMS coaches before leaving Wendover at 8.45 pm. Men were to be posted at all crossing gates to ensure that they remained open for the special. Departing from Wendover at 9.33 pm the train was scheduled to arrive at Marylebone at 10.27 pm (which it did) and subsequently the empty LMS stock would be moved to Acton Wells with the LMS pilotman.

In order to simplify operation of the Chesham branch in 1941, some of the old Ashbury coaches held in the wartime strategic store had been used to form a shuttle hauled by some ex-GCR 9K's, which were fitted for auto-vacuum working. This avoided the need to run-round the train at the end of each trip.

The London end of the Joint was the main target for bombing. Inevitably the Met facilities in the City were badly damaged and Baker Street station suffered a direct hit. Marylebone was also put out of action and for some months trains were terminated at Neasden, where a temporary platform built from sleepers was erected. Some bombs were dropped all along the Joint either by intent, or by indiscriminate dumping. Then in the last phase of the war V1 flying bombs fell on Marylebone, Lord's tunnel, Wembley Park and later the V2 rockets landed on Neasden and elsewhere. The remaining Met locos with LT had to be pressed into service and some Met locos now owned by the LNER, such as the G class now returned to operating trains beyond Rickmansworth.

As the war dragged on the state of the Joint steadily deteriorated due to the combined effect of enemy action, shortages of vital materials (such as coal), staff, and the cumulative lack of maintenance. Probably the provision of adequate locomotive power was hardest hit and a vignette in the next chapter illustrates the dire straits that existed at that time and the determination to keep going. Whilst it became a battle just to run the trains, the occasional outstanding performance was still achieved and in 1944 Cecil J Allen noted such a run behind an A3 'Minoru' with 13 coaches of 405 tons tare and 425 loaded which left Marylebone at 3.30pm. "From the start we passed Kilburn, 3 miles in 7min 57sec, with a minimum speed of 28mph on the last mile at 1 in 100-95; over Neasden Junction we slowed to 45mph – a common practice recently – but reached Harrow, 9.2 miles in 16min 10sec. The 15min schedule is very tight for a load of over 400 tons. From Harrow to Rickmansworth we were badly checked by signals, and so passed the latter station at 30mph, with the 6 mile climb to Amersham, almost all at 1 in 105 immediately ahead. Now Minoru was opened out to some purpose, and the Buckinghamshire uplands resounded to the engine's vocal efforts as we slowly accelerated to 36mph at Chorley Wood, 39mph at Chalfont, and then to precisely 40 mph. The 8 miles from Harrow to Rickmansworth took 15min 30sec, but then the 6.4 miles from there up to Amersham were completed in 10min 41sec – a very fine piece of work. Before Great Missenden we touched 70½ mph: then came what seems almost inevitable on this train – a dead slow for signals at Wendover. Almost every day it occurs; either here ,at Great Missenden or Dutchlands intermediate "home"; and in addition the train is kept waiting at Aylesbury for the GW connection. Our time for the 37.4 miles from Marylebone was 44min 25sec, ½ min less than the 45min allowed, but the net time was nearer 37min. Waiting for the connection took us 10min instead of the booked 3min, and we left 7min late. The run of 21.4 miles to Brackley was then made in 25min 18sec, with 65mph attained at Grendon and again beyond Calvert, a minimum of 52mph at 1 in 176 past Finmere some 16.6miles in 20min 2sec. A signal check prevented any further gain to Woodford and the 9.8 miles to Brackley on a 1 in 176 grade took 15min 23sec. On reaching Leicester the crew had a gain of at least 16min."

However, even before the end of the war thoughts turned to how the railways would be developed. The existing railway companies produced their own plans for the post-war era, but these were used to fend off the inevitable threat of nationalisation and bolster credibility in order to obtain the maximum compensation. The Government commissioned a Report by Sir Charles Inglis which recommended a 30yr £230M programme to develop the railways of London by a series of deep mainline tunnels, including Baker Street – Clapham Junction and Marylebone – Holborn Viaduct *(shades of Crossrail!)* But the reality was somewhat different because the basic infrastructure of the railways had been seriously degraded by lack of maintenance and investment, compounded by shortages of fuel and the cheap labour on which they depended. In like manner the competitive position of the motor vehicle had actually been improved by the war. In retrospect the depravations of the war almost mortally wounded the railways and when a Labour Government was swept to power in 1945, nationalisation became inescapable. The old 'Big Four' & LT briefly flickered into a last show of initiatives on the way they would have developed with brochures, exhibitions, new liveries (including some new LNER L1 locos now on the Joint), renumbering and new forms of traction such as gas turbine & diesel. However this had little practical effect on the regime to come.

ooooOooooo

90

CHAPTER 9

VIGNETTES

Sir Edward Watkin in action during a Met half-yearly shareholders meeting on 24th January 1891 (with acknowledgements to F Cockman Esq.).

Sir Edward: *'In connection with the extension of the MS&LR to London you are going to obtain for your 42 miles of the Metropolitan a large and new system of traffic on which the MS&L will pay you 66 2/3rds of all the traffic they carry over those 42 miles'.*

Mr Snowden: 'Is the Metropolitan capital implicated?'

Sir Edward: *'Not a farthing - I told you so before!'.*

Shareholder: 'Is there any guarantee the M&SL will not compete with the Met?'.

Sir Edward: *'This is absurd and ridiculous. Have you anything else to say or any sense to utter?'.*

Mr Spring: 'I entered the room at 12 o'clock and found the report had been carried. We know nothing about the MS&L Bill'.

Sir Edward: *'I have explained this on six separate occasions before, and Mr Spring does not understand it because he does not want to understand it'.*

Mr Spring: 'I am here as a small shareholder - my stock is £2,000, but my stock is as much to me as £60,000 to Sir Edward Watkin. He may be autocratic and denounce a poor shareholder but from what I read in the paper there will be a good deal of opposition to it'.

Sir Edward: *'I knew he would head the opposition, I knew he would!'.*

Mr Spring: 'I am a shareholder in other lines but I have never met with a gentleman who behaves in the autocratic way that Sir Edward Watkin does in the Chair. I always meet with respect at meetings I attend. If I travel with the Chairman so well and good, but if not, I am open to abuse'.

Shareholder: 'Passengers are continually in the habit of riding first class with a third class ticket'.

Sir Edward: *'We have put on extra inspectors to stop this practice'.*

Bob Clark, a Joint stationman: As a boy he applied for a job at Chesham station and, as it was their turn to recruit, he was sent to the LNER at Hamilton Place in London to be interviewed and given a medical. Bob started on the 6th May 1935 as a parcel delivery boy at Chesham for £1 pw together with a Joint uniform. He started at 4am sorting parcels and the 5am newspaper train was the first to be dealt with and then the 'shuttle' went into action, followed by loading the van for the 8.30am to Marylebone and thence to the north. Regular traffic included racing pigeons for release several miles away, which had to be collected from the Golden Ball pub, and when in season the wicker baskets of cress from the River Chess. Under the watchful eye of the guard, Harry 'ding-dong' Bell they had to be stacked in a precise order for onward transport by the 'big four'. Once a tank loco whilst shunting the van in the yard ran away and embedded itself in the dead end under Punchbowl Lane bridge. The Pullman trains also broke the routine, particularly on one occasion when the buffers locked with another coach in the yard and a gang had to come out from Neasden with a hydraulic jack to clear it.

In 1939 Bob took a relief parcel office/platform post at Northwood. At that time 'relief' posts were expected to be prepared if necessary to work on their home companies system. So in Bob's case this could mean anywhere on the old GCR, even Leicester. War had just broken out and a number of units were stationed in the area, including the HQ of Coastal Command, which the Germans tried to bomb. A company of the Irish Guards was also nearby and took over the goods shed for their stores. Train operations were made more difficult by the Air Raid Precautions which included the dimming of all lights, even the automatic signalling, to the extent that one day an express headed by the A4 'Dominion of Canada' came to a halt in the station. However worse was to happen when a platoon of soldiers were crossing from one platform to the other hauling a station trolley piled high with their kitbags. Unfortunately this got stuck in the tracks and the troops had to watch helplessly as an express ploughed its way right through, scattering their kit everywhere.

Bob moved next to Rickmansworth in 1941 where the goods yard was full of aircraft components and the goods shed contained the strategic supply of corned beef. Here he was expected to assist with the changeover between steam and electric traction where one man dealt with the vacuum pipes plus couplings and the other connecting the jumper cables. For replenishing the steam locos some 6 wagons of coal were delivered each week. Memorably he recalls an express, complete with destination boards on the coaches, going through the station , which is restricted to a maximum of 25 mph, at a speed well in excess of 50 mph accompanied by much squealing of flanges on the rails. 1942 saw Bob move to Amersham, where amongst the daily passengers were a number of small London shopkeepers who, because of the bombing, brought home their valuable stock each night. However soon the scene became dominated by soldiers based in the vicinity. Troop trains became common and on one day a huge 17 coach train arrived, which had needed two guards as it had to pull up twice at the platform. The American 5th Division established a number of local camps at Pipers Wood and elsewhere and these provided much excitement when the men returned from an evening visit to London. They would be met at the station by an array of US Army

George White, the parcels van driver based at Amersham in the 30's, beside his 1928 Thornycroft which had been borrowed from the Watford branch - thus the sign 'Metro & LNERlys'. He was well known by collecting the 'luggage in advance' in the district. On retirement he kept close to the Joint by running the bookstall at Chalfont. *(R Hardy)*

Bill Parsons, the lengthman, with the rest of the Amersham pw gang at the south end of the station around 1937. They could detect the smallest alignment problem by eye and maintained their track from Rectory Hill to Bell Lane at Chalfont in tip top condition. They knew the drivers would certainly complain if they did not. *(R Hardy)*

A Robinson designed 9Q that was perpetuated by the LNER, No.5482 a 4 cylinder 4-6-0 now a B7, which tended to work the piped goods to Manchester, excursions and other specials that needed real power. Here Driver George Park is in charge of an up train at Harrow in 1937, whilst the new LT station arises in the background. *(Richard Hardy)*

Usually on Sunday mornings in the 1930's some three excursions would leave Marylebone within 15 mins for Nottingham & Sheffield, each with 12 coaches, for a 7/9d return fare. Pictured is 'Lord Stuart of Wortley', a Caprotti geared LNER class B3, thrashing past the new Weller Met estate, south of Amersham. *(Richard Hardy)*

The 16.06 ex-Amersham for Marylebone in 1939, with the safety valve blowing-off on no.5506, an 'improved' GCR Director, now a LNER class D11. At this time the words '& Chesham Bois' had been added to the Amersham station nameboard - although it was possible to reach it both from Chesham and Chalfont & Latimer. *(Richard Hardy)*

Again at Amersham, in 1940 after the outbreak of the war, and no.6166 'Earl Haig', with Caprotti poppet valve gear, awaits to leave with the 08.15 Marylebone - Leicester train. Fireman Ted Manion is with Driver Ted Simpson who came from Liverpool in 1899 to open the GCR service to London. *(Richard Hardy)*

A Sunday excursion express from Marylebone, headed by an LNER class B3, thundering at speed towards the southern end of Amersham station. On the right is the Met signal box and in the background the new MetroLand estate. *(Richard Hardy)*

The Halton light railway was built in 1917 from Wendover station on the Joint to serve the large military camp on the nearby Rothschild estate. It became an RAF base and expanded in the Second War. This rare photo of about 1936 near the Aylesbury road shows one of the original 0-6-0T engines used on the branch. *(Clive Foxell Collection)*

The Halton Light Railway

Standard gauge 1917-63 ——————
2ft gauge, removed 1941 — — — — —

Scale: ½ mile

The Halton light railway originated from a proposal by the Wendover station master. The layout of the standard gauge lines is shown above, together with a 2ft gauge extension across the Icknield Way into the beech woods on slopes of the Chilterns.

A LNER class A5 ex-GCrab 4-6-2T no.5024 heading a down Marylebone to Aylesbury train near Chorley Wood. *(Patrick O'Hind)*

An early morning Chesham to Liverpool St. fast train in May 1947. It has been hauled from Rickmansworth by electric loco no.1, whose nameplates - 'John Lyon' - had been removed during the war. Looking from this vantage point at North Harrow station one could see how the Bo-Bo's at speed seemed to snake along the track. *(Patrick O'Hind)*

A 1927 aerial photo of Harrow on the Hill looking to the north. Joint jurisdiction began at the signal box to the bottom-left of Station Road bridge (in the middle): to the right are the redundant loco exchange sidings. Above the station is the Met power station on the left and in the distance are the Uxbridge branch and the goods yard. *(Aerofilms)*

99

An aerial picture of Aylesbury Joint station in 1954 looking south. The tripartite loco shed is on the right, with a GW 'Prairie' tank which worked their line curving to the right to Princes Risborough. At the top an N5 is by the signal box (site of the 1904 crash). And in the bay platform the next LT train waits to leave for the City. *(Aerofilms)*

military policemen (in white helmets and thus known as 'snowdrops') waiting to give any recalcitrant a swift blow with the long baton they carried. However some soldiers just jumped out of the other side of the coaches and ran off up the track back to base.

Bob also did a turn at Chalfont & Latimer near where Bertram Mills Circus had their winter quarters. The circus moved mainly by train and on one occasion an elephant put a foot through the flooring of the GWR 'monster' van that it was travelling in. The station master used to charge the local people to watch the animals being unloaded, whilst a ganger collected the inevitable manure for his allotment. Other characters included Dorothy Paget the well-known racehorse owner who came up to the station most days for the 10.25 am ex-Marylebone to receive a message from her trainer with the latest tips. The diplomat Sir Ivone Kirkpartrick was a frequent traveller and remembered because he usually gave a generous tip of 2/6d. Bob also recalls the last Hunt that was brought by rail to Chalfont & Latimer, but some of the last animals to be dealt with were a van of donkeys for a local dealer to which some wag had attached a placard that read 'another bunch of railway recruits'!

Ending his time at Amersham, Bob sometimes shared duties with a relief stationman, Bob Butcher, who also had worked all along the Joint. Once at Quainton Road he had witnessed a wagon that had been loose-shunted rather powerfully run away to the mainline, where it derailed and was struck by a passing N5 loco, luckily without serious damage. Bob Clark also admired the way in which the local ticket inspector, Ernie Woodstock, could trap devious passengers who tried to avoid paying for a ticket. Their favourite ruse was lurk in the toilet until the coast seemed clear and then make a run for it – but Ernie always got them. Bob finally retired in 1985 after 50 years service.

Oswald S Nock remembers a pre-war footplate journey on the 'Newspaper flyer' in 1936. (with due acknowledgement)
'The mere sight of the ordinary placid Marylebone struck an immediate note of urgency, as lorry after lorry dashed in from Fleet Street; and before 2 am many of the vans of the train were piled literally to the roof with newspapers. The departure time, 2.32 am is symbolic of a service that is timed, verily to the last half minute. The train on this occasion consisted of 8 newspaper vans and 1 passenger coach, 271 tons tare, and 300 tons loaded; for an ordinary GC service with a 'Sandringham' to haul it, this would have been just a nice running load, but on the 'Newspaper', there proved precious little time to spare. No.2841 Gayton Hall was the engine, with Driver E Simpson and Fireman J Wood in charge. She was in good condition, and riding well, so much so that during the actual trip the sheer thrill of speed tended to eclipse the technical excellence of the working.

2.30 am! A last van raced into the station. Stacks of papers were loaded like lightning, and then on the stroke of 2.32 the van doors were slammed; a green light shone far down the platform, and we were off. There is no need to humour the 'Sandringhams' in starting away, they can be 'given the lot' at once, and on a fine night and a dry rail No.2841 fairly lifted the train out of Marylebone. Linking-up began almost at once, and on entering the tunnel under Lord's cricket ground , a half a mile from the start, Simpson had pulled up to 35% cut-off. Through this tunnel, and the succeeding one under St. John's Wood the driver was continually applying sand; but there was no slipping, and in the short break where the line crosses the LMS main line from Euston, Simpson linked up further to 25%. Up the 1 in 100 to the summit near Brondesbury we sustained 32mph, and on passing this point, 3 miles out, cut-off was reduced to a minimum.

Accelerating swiftly through the sleeping suburbs we were doing 70mph through Neasden, and then sustained a truly tearing pace over the sharply undulating track through MetroLand: 53 up Harrow, 66 at Pinner, 59 over Northwood crest , and no less than 75½ mph at Watford South Junction. We braked hard for Rickmansworth, coming right down to 25mph, but the moment we were round the north curve Simpson opened out to full regulator, and 25% cut-off. Already we were a ahead of time but the heavy climb to Amersham following immediately upon the severe slowing through Rickmansworth pulled down the average speed. With cut-off further advanced to 30% we gathered speed steadily, passing Chorley Wood at 35mph and we forged our way up amongst the glorious beech woods of the Chiltern Hills. It was a very dark night; the sky was overcast, there was no moon yet, and the nearness of the trees on either side made it seem almost like a tunnel, save when an occasional branch or tree trunk was illuminated by the light from the fire. On the upper part of the climb the speed was sustained at 36mph, and in 31¾ mins we had breasted Amersham summit, 23.6 miles from Marylebone. Here the reverser was adjusted back to the 15% position, and thus it remained unchanged on to Brackley.

Very soon we were making some terrific speed; touching 77mph before Great Missenden, we were over Dutchlands at 63, and then went pell-mell down to Aylesbury. The regulator remained full open until we reached 80mph but then it was almost closed. I have many times been thrilled on the footplate, but have never known the equal of this – tearing downhill on a pitch black night at 84mph, without a glimmer of light ahead, either from the track or the surrounding country. Approaching Aylesbury steam was shut right off, a very slight application of the brake was made to steady the train round the curve, and with a scream of the whistle we swept through. Such, however, is the booked time that despite this magnificent running of Gayton Hall we were 13 secs *late* through Aylesbury – 44 mins 13 secs for the 37.9 miles from Marylebone. Speed was eased to 55mph over Quainton Road Junction but then with the regulator full open again we ran so fast to cover the concluding uphill stretch from Grendon Junction to stop at Brackley at an average of exactly 60mph. Beyond Calvert we touched 71mph; the 4¾ miles of Finmere bank were cleared at 61½mph, and an acceleration to 73mph in 1½ miles (!) put the finishing touch to reach Brackley (59.3 miles) some 2 mins early, in 64¾ mins from Marylebone.'

As a young man John Parnham was a surveyor working on the Joint between Pinner and Rickmansworth in the 1930's. At this time the electrification had reached Watford and although the new T stock had been introduced, there were still a number of the old Ashbury and the 1905 multiple electric stock in use. A set of the latter was always stabled at Harrow overnight and on one occasion a compressor was left running, became overheated and burnt the coach out.

John was often working near the primitive Moor Park & Sandy Lodge station due to problems with the embankments. One Saturday he wanted to get to the nearby platelayer's lobby where his things were kept, but the driver of his train overshot the platform and John realised all he had to do was to get on to the running board and jump down onto the trackside near the hut. However, having shut the door behind him he found that his coat was caught - so the driver had to come and release him. The driver's grumbling was counterbalanced by the platelayers comments that it was he who had forgotten to stop at the station.

Another incident at this spot concerned Frankie Coleman who was one of the top 'flaggies' of the Met. Needless to say there was a severe speed restriction where the gang was working to the south of Moor Park, when a roar like thunder was heard from the direction of Northwood and a big'un came down upon them going full tilt. Frankie just gave a flash of his red flag to bring the driver to his senses before the bend at Ricky, but too late and the driver ground to a halt - so that the very well-built Frankie had to run to Moor Park to give the driver the green flag.

Whilst surveying John noticed that the standard length of the refuge sidings accommodated just 40 wagons plus engine and brake van. Indeed sometimes Met drivers had to compress the buffers against the van hand brake in order to get in, however one day it all seemed too easy - until the crew found that they had demolished the bufferstop! He never understood how a typical longer GCR goods train could have used these sidings, but perhaps at night they had a clear path.

The frequent slips of the nearby clay cuttings were an ongoing problem, but finally drastic action was taken by loading the slopes with fuel and burning it to consolidate the soil. When the gang were working in the vicinity, Lord Ebury's gamekeeper (who liked his morning pint) used to ask them to keep an eye on things. However the gang turned beaters and drove the birds from the woods across the track when they saw a train coming. If the birds co-operated they flew at such a level that they hit the engine and conveniently fell beside the track. The gang felt that they were entitled to do this as Lord Ebury did not have game rights over the Joint! John also reports that the rabbit pie was excellent - if well cooked.

There was always something different about Ricky and certainly it was a source of many incidents. One arose when one of the colourful Met drivers, Barratt, was in charge of the 'Chiltern Flyer'. This was the crack Met train which ran non-stop between Amersham to Harrow and was the only Met train to carry an express headcode. It also carried a guard at each end and one teased Barratt that he was scared of the curve through Ricky station. On that day the passengers were waiting at Ricky for the following train when they heard such a roar from the north that they dived for cover as the 'Flyer' shot round the bend. On reaching Harrow, and handing the train over to a Bo-Bo electric loco, Barratt returned straight to Neasden Shed where he was met by an irate Superintendent with the words "Now Barratt don't do that again; we don't want to frighten the passengers". The reason that he and others could get through Ricky at well over the 25mph limit was that the track was set deliberately out of gauge by the Met platelayers but with the incorporation into LT responsibility moved to the District at Lillie Bridge. They insisted that the track be slewed to the LT standard dimensions but when the next ex GCR big'un came through it left behind most of its running boards!

The following description of life at the LNER Neasden engine shed after the absorption of the Met locos in 1937 is transcribed from contemporary notes made by Ron Eagles and Frank Smith.

Frank Smith had an uncle who worked at Neasden and as a result of the earlier Depression it imbued him with the thought that "get a job on the railways and you have a job for life". Thus he applied for a position as a cleaner in 1937 and was interviewed by Matthew Robinson, Area Superintendent and son of the great 'J G', and started at 15/- pw. He began at the bottom with the cleaner's gang, where there were two shifts of 10 men starting at 6am & 2pm together with 12 men who rotated between 6am, 2pm & 10pm. Each shift was led by one of the 3 foremen, of which Fred Woodman was confusingly an identical twin of Tommy a driver. They gathered in a dark brick-built & cavernous mess room for a brew-up and on his way to sign on for work Tommy would peer through the grimy window, pretending to be Fred, producing a sudden exodus and much bad language.

Work was allocated by the foreman on the basis of seniority, starting with the most lowly, but clean job, of 'knocking-up' the footplate crew an hour before duty from midnight to 6am. Next would be the cleaning groups, which often tossed a coin to decide who would clean the difficult parts of the engine and the best jobs would be given for labouring, tube sweeping and cleaning the toilets-although these jobs might be dirty it meant that they were ready for promotion.

In 1938 Frank was made redundant along with many other cleaners due to the economic situation, however as war loomed he was recalled and looked towards a footplate job. The first step would be on the Relief Link which involved turns on shed such as coaling, disposing & preparation of the engines but with the prospect of covering for men who failed to report for duty. Men who had failed their medical checks also covered for this and any pilot duties. The next step was the Coal Train Link of 8-10 turns before the three Local Train Links which averaged 9 crews per link. One of these was known as the 'hungry nine' where men stayed on it until retirement, unless removed by the LNER medical officer. The No.2, or Fast Goods was known as the Pipe Train Link which included the Manchester Goods amongst its 5 turns. But everybody's ambition was the Top Link of 5 turns including the: Night Mail: 3.30pm Manchester: Early Newspaper 2.32am Marylebone - 4.55am Leicester - 7.43am return: 10.00am Down and the drivers at that time were G.Parks, F.France then J.Fisher, E.Simpson & Palphreyman then J.Docks. (Simpson and Palphreyman both lost sons in railway accidents.)

In 1937 a number of Met crews transferred to the LNER shed, but some went back on LT ballast work. They had different agreements to the LNER men and their own union negotiations. They tended to operate the lower links in which there were about 18 passenger turns and 16 goods turns. In the absence of the Met drivers their place was taken by Met passed firemen and then by LNER firemen. Eventually by natural wastage and transfers back to LT, all the Neasden turns were undertaken by LNER men.

For passenger workings the Met men worked from Rickmansworth to Aylesbury. The train had been hauled from the City or Baker Street by an electric loco which was uncoupled and went into a siding ready for its next trip on the up line back to London. Their steam loco stood in a little siding with a small pit, coaling stage and a nearby water column, as the loco's tanks were always filled before going into the siding. With the coupling of the steam loco the train proceeded to Chesham or Aylesbury and sometimes to Quainton Road. The Met Trains seemed lighter than the LNER ones did but they had difficulty starting a train from 'cold' with an unknown degree of vacuum and little chance to superheat. In consequence they rarely left without a degree of slipping. The amount of water in the boiler was also different by the time the train reached Chorley Wood and after then many a firemen pulled the top cock of the water gauge more frequently than a barman in a busy pub! There were times when the trips were comfortable, but in the main they were a struggle to maintain water and steam, with a lot of coal being shovelled. By comparison the heavier LNER trains were better sprung and with an A5 having run in all the way from Marylebone, it made light work of pulling out on the curve for the climb to Amersham.

The main Met goods workings started from Harrow Yard and were taken to Neasden, Willesden Green and Finchley Road with a transfer road to the Midland Railway. Coal trains were worked to Neasden LT power station and also South Harrow which was taken via the Uxbridge line to Rayners Lane and back up the Piccadilly line to the gas works. The Uxbridge line was also covered as were the Extension line yards at Pinner, Northwood, Watford and all the yards from Rickmansworth to Quainton Road. There was also a yard at Verney Junction which was reached on the single line from Quainton Rd. and where transfers were made to LMS Oxford-Cambridge line. Most of the yards were small and shunting was accomplished by going in several times to remove the empties. There was a vast difference in working such steam goods trains over the electric tracks for the distance between signals was shorter and on some routes a red signal could follow a green, as there were no distant signals.

The Neasden drivers came from all over the country, some from the north with the opening of the GCR. They were all types: Bill Reynolds a fireman who could rival any comedian, Driver Fred Waite an expert in stocks and shares, others knowledgeable on gardening, rabbits, jazz and beer. All had different personalities but with a sense of responsibility and self discipline to match their craft, they created the tone of the depot. Although banter was the order of the day, there was also mutual respect between cleaner, driver and foreman. "Neasden was the best"

The following is a short transcript of the diary of the Neasden Shed Foreman, Bill Harvey for 1944/5 which shows what it was really like! As the war drew to a close the conditions on the Joint due to shortages of labour & materials got even worse – then to be compounded by the terrible weather.

24 April 1944 – General Manager tells me to 'go to Neasden to put it right'. Matt Robinson *(Depot Supt. and son of 'JG', who had suffered in the First War and who had just lost his disabled son)* seemed distinctly annoyed by this. Discussed the difficulty of lifting the USA locos with shear legs. *(US Army 2-8-0 engines built to the European loading gauge & some 2700 were sent to the Continent)*

28 April – Went to Neasden and inspected the perforated oil pipes on USA 2050.

11 May – to Neasden to investigate various loco problems; 5260 L.F. eccentric broken, 4830 R. combination lever broken, 4812 MBE running hot.

6 June – D-day!

28 June – V1 flying bomb has landed on Lords tunnel.

3 July – Go to Peterborough to inspect collapsed intermediate rubbing blocks on WD Austerity locos.

11 July – Post haste to Neasden to find 23 engines stopped, including 14 USA's with hot boxes.

14 July – Post haste to Woodford regarding their overheating problems on USA's.

15 July – Reported to the General Manager that our examiners are being misled by the high running temperatures of the bronze bearings into thinking that this is abnormal. Instructed to go to Neasden and examine all 14 USA's. Released 5 still warm and the rest after checking pads and journals.

26 July – Matt off sick and find Neasden in a hell of a mess with 22 engines stopped. Both wheel drop tables broken and less than one days supply of coal left.

31 July – Am Acting Superintendent until Matt resumes. 30 engines stopped.

2 August – 27 engines stopped. Driver refused to take a Canadian Transportation Corps soldier as a fireman, so suspended him.

4 August – 22 engines stopped. Hospital special 29 mins late away when coaling and GM livid.

5 August – 19 engines stopped. Ran out of coal at 4.30 am. Got 2 ashmen to fill wagons from stack with steam crane and ash elevator.

6 August – No buses at 6.30 am so walked to work arriving at 9.30 am

9 August – 24 'casuals' picked up 80 tons of coal but hopper ran out during night & 4 trains cancelled. Coal only coming in driblets.

13 August - Only hours of coal left and 5336 derailed under coaling plant.

15 August – coaling plant stopped due to seized eccentric, now having to load manually and tank engines coaling in London. First squad of Italian POW's arrive to help with coaling.

19 August – Rain, and loco of Ambulance train blocked by empty coal wagons. Coaling at Marylebone stops due to hoist failure.

21 August – Matt back. No fireman for Ambulance train. Air Raid so foreman lights up fires in engines on his own. Avalanche of accident reports.

8 September – Firebox collapses of USA 1707 . Blackout ceases and Home Guard parades are now voluntary. First supersonic V2 rocket falls on Chiswick, heard a violent explosion followed by a whistling noise.

22 November – told to see 'absentees and encourage them to return to work'.

26 November – start staying at Neasden overnight to ensure punctual morning departures. USA 7076 stopped with 2 ft of flange broken off from tender wheel.

13 December – Fog & no buses. Trains cancelled due to 17 absentees. Italian NCO difficult. Kings Cross asking for shovels so sent 12. LT to strike at Xmas.

23 December – 6338 failed at Northolt and 5276 whilst being turned collided the with the North Circular Road bridge displacing the gas main.

11 January 1945 – Italian POW knocked down and seriously injured when an engine collided with the ash elevator.

13/18 January – 6 engines stopped. V2 rocket landed at Hornsey. K3 no. 3814 working a special petrol train collided with an electric train at Rickmansworth. Italian POW's out of control.

29 January – Prolonged frost and sub-zero temperatures. 5505 frozen cylinders.

9/10 February – 6 in water main burst and no water available on shed, but later found due to closure of wrong valve.

21 February – 9.50 late again as wrong oil put in lubricator.

2 March – WD 77364 derailed all wheels at entrance to shed and borrowed the Met 30 ton crane to re-rail it. Last train gone so slept in office.

12 March - Will just scrape through for coal. 3 LT trains cancelled.

16 March – V2 rocket lands on Neasden Circus and poor (*Driver*) Copperthwaite is badly injured and his wife killed.

2 April – Right out of coal and hopper is empty. Dislodged residue with a hand grenade taken from the Home Guard stores. *(Special coal train arrived next day)*

5 April – Magneto stolen from hired ash elevator. Bardsley arrived to take over.

9/10 April – All ok at shed and took Bardsley around the district, riding 5030 to High Wycombe, 5917 to Aylesbury and 1355 to call in at Chesham. Next day bright and sunny but not best pleased to be back in the pandemonium of Craighead. G M sent for me – no prospect of promotion until after the war.

oooo000ooooo

The Joint became part of BR upon the nationalisation of the railways in 1948. Apart from the use of different signs and numbers things remained much the same at first, as witnessed by a now BR no.69259 2MT ex-LNE N5 built by Parker of the MS&L in 1891, here taking water at Aylesbury for the Princes Risborough -Quainton shuttle.*(RH)*

Still in relatively fresh LNER liveries in June1948, one of Gresley's popular B1 4-6-0 no.1164 pilots another numbered 1185 on an up Manchester - Marylebone express just passing Moor Park siding. This was still surrounded by bridge girders that had delivered before the war, ready for the LT electrification programme. *(Ken Nunn/LCGB)*

Also in 1948, BR undertook a series of locomotive exchanges to determine the best of the existing types. The tests for mixed-traffic engines took place over the Joint with similar loads. Here the ex-GWR 4-6-0 'Witherslack Hall' with dynamometer car behind is passing through Northwood on the 23rd June. The results were inconclusive. *(GCRS)*

The original 1892 Met signal box at the south end of Amersham station, built to a similar design as most on the Extension, it is painted in the post-war LT scheme of grey and cream. Originally a Saxby 24 lever frame, the starting signal was interlocked with the next box in order to control the departure times. *(Tony Geary)*

Around 1950 a Willesden-bound freight plods past the south of Rickmansworth yard hauled by an ex-Ministry of Supply 'Austerity' 2-8-0 designed by Riddles, no.90180, and purchased by BR in 1948. *(Stephen Gradidge)*

The 1950's saw the gradual rundown under Eastern Region of longer-distance steam services on the Joint. But Gresley 2-6-0 V2's were in wide use and here no.60961 works an up Woodford-Marylebone local train under the bridge to the Watford triangle, between the branch and the mainline. *(Stephen Gradidge)*

The gravel pits between Moor Park & Rickmansworth had been worked since the construction of the Extension, but in later years were used as tips. LT owned one near the Watford triangle and here in 1956 the usual Met locos were being replace by ex-GWR pannier tanks, in this case no.5752 which has become L91. *(Stephen Gradidge)*

By the early 1950's the newer Thompson 2-6-4T's began to replace the traditional GCrabs on the ex-Met and LNER local services. Here in 1956 a group of four L1's are pictured at rest inside the gloom of Neasden ER shed. *(Pendon)*

The afternoon up parcels train for Marylebone in 1956, hauled by BR 2-6-0 class 4 no.76041, passing under the original footbridge at the primitive Moor Park station. The responsibility for the Joint services from Marylebone was to transfer from Eastern to London Midland Region of BR, with a further loss of services. *(Stephen Gradidge)*

In 1956 two named expresses with restaurant cars were reintroduced from Marylebone, and this picture shows the 'Master Cutler' from Sheffield. B1 4-6-0's and A3 pacific's were often used and no.60104 snakes round the Rickmansworth curve. But the sound of real expresses pounding over the Chilterns was to be short-lived. *(Stephen Gradidge)*

CHAPTER 10

NATIONALSATION

The last timetable of the Joint was issued on the 6th October1947 with the cover bearing the dual LNER 'lozenge' and LT 'bull's-eye' logos. The transport system of the UK was nationalised on the 1st January1948 under the British Transport Commission controlling 5 Executives for Railways, London Transport, Hotels, Docks & Waterways and Road Transport. Whilst senior positions were 'shuffled' between the former constituents, at working level it took some time before most noticed much difference. The Joint had formally ceased to exist but again two separate executive bodies – LTE and BR(Eastern Region) still had to share the line. This continued in the pragmatic manner that had been evolved during the war with perhaps less emphasis on disputing minutae of financial matters now that both were under the same accounting umbrella.

Inevitably the thrust of BR was to standardise across their railway system on best practice in equipment and operations in order to achieve greater efficiency. However the infrastructure that they had inherited reflected the need to match the local conditions. A classic example was the desire to determine the 'best' locomotive designs so that these features could be employed as the basis for a new range of standard BR engines, without fully recognising that the Big Four and their predecessors had built them originally to match their terrain and local supplies of coal and water. Nevertheless BR embarked in 1948 on a series of trials of the main existing locomotive types and those tests for mixed traffic class engines took place over the Joint. It was assumed that the characteristics of the 'home' engines were well-known and therefore the formal trials were restricted to representatives from the rest of the 'Big Four' companies namely: 'Bude' no.34006 a SR West Country Pacific, an LMS class 5 4-6-0 no.45253 and 'Witherslack Hall' a GWR 4-6-0 no.6990. They took place in the aftermath of the war in June 1948 with loads of 380 to 395 tons, including the dynamometer car. With the number of permanent way restrictions near to London plus signal delays due to the inevitable problems of congestion between Harrow and Rickmansworth, it was difficult to draw any general conclusions at this point. The table below shows their performance thereafter to Aylesbury where Bude achieved a speed of 51mph over Dutchlands Summit and then 60-70mph downhill, the Class 5 60-62mph and the Hall some 60mph. Next across the Vale of Aylesbury, 'Bude' sustained a spell at 69-70mph, the Class 5 some 60-62mph and the Hall a period at 60mph.

Section	SR 'Bude'	LMS Class 5	GWR 'Hall'
Rickm'th - Aylesbury	25m 48s	32m 37s	31m 21s
Scheduled at 26mins.			
Aylesbury - Woodford	31m 24s	36m 24s	37m 07s
Scheduled at 35 mins.			

Bearing in mind the unfamiliar 'road' and coal as well as different driving techniques, all the engines performed satisfactorily. Indeed it is difficult to draw any overall conclusions except, as might be expected, the larger and more powerful 'Bude' exhibited notable acceleration characteristics.

On more routine matters the services on the Joint reverted to the basic pre-war pattern, but with ever-ageing stock. For the LT the semi-fast trains continued with the multiple-electric T stock and the fast ones with the Bo-Bo electric locos hauling the venerable Dreadnought coaches but lacking the frills, such as first class and the Met Pullmans. The Met spirit was still alive though, for in 1951 a detailed proposal was put to the LT Operating Committee that a new refreshment car service be introduced to Aylesbury. However, it was considered that little revenue would be generated and it could therefore be only justified for goodwill and publicity and so the decision was "*I do not think that we are the right people for a stunt of this nature – not even the Met*"! Onwards from Rickmansworth the local trains were hauled by the ex GC C13 4-4-2T's and N5 0-6-2T's, with an occasional ex GER N7 0-6-2T. Such were the magnitude of problems at Neasden that LT often provided a standby engine at Rickmansworth, often in the form of an Met E class tank, which still seemed to be able to handle the load, if needed.

The significant goods workings from the old GCR, which had been built-up during the war, remained concentrated on the Wycombe route, but the Joint continued to provide a welcome relief path for these and a expanding range of specials which included the 'Motorail', sleeper and 'Starlight' services to Scotland, as well as the old mail and newspaper trains. After the war the semi-fast local trains from Marylebone continued to be dealt with by the ex GCR 4-4-0 Director's and 4-4-2 Atlantic's with the locals hauled by the ex GC A5 2-6-4T's and then later by the newer ex LNER Thompson L1 2-6-4T's. For the longer runs to Woodford the B1 4-6-0's and soon V2 2-6-2's became the order of day. Odd exceptions were two slow stopping trains: the 07.45 Marylebone-Leicester and the 13.12 Nottingham-Marylebone often in charge of a B1 or an A3 4-6-2, which were referred to by the old tag for a 'stopping all stations' train – the 'Parliamentary'. Then during 1958 two named expresses with restaurant cars were revived, the up 'Master Cutler' which took about 3½ hrs for the journey to Sheffield and the 'South Yorkshireman' to Bradford. These were usually headed by A3's, or sometimes B1's, and once again the Joint was the scene for powerful trains blasting their way over the Chilterns. Sadly this resurgence was only to last for about a year for the continual changes at the top of BR were to have serious ramifications for the Joint. Firstly, in the late 1950's an overall review of competing routes suggested a major down grading of this line and the this was quickly followed by the surprising transfer of responsibility for the 'Joint' from Eastern Region to the London Midland Region of BR. They inevitably seized the opportunity to implement the outcome of earlier review to reduce services to the minimum. Ironically at this time the Joint became extremely useful as a diversionary route for the LMR as a result of the restrictions at Euston due to the rebuilding and electrification works. Although in 1961 there were still some 10 semi-fast trains a day from Marylebone to Woodford (and a few beyond), by the next year this fell to just 3: a level that would before long eventually self-justify closure. Neasden Engine Shed was closed in 1962 and local trains were taken over mainly by Ivatt and Fairburn tank engines based at Willesden, together with a wide variety of visitors, such as the ex LMS Fowler 2-6-4T's, which from their low profile were nicknamed 'surface raiders'. In the last phase of steam operation BR standard engines such as 2MT, 4MT, 5MT, 9F's and Britannia's together with a number of 4-6-0 'Black 5's came to predominate, although a few of other types such as K3's and Royal Scots did appear.

All this was in complete contrast to the approach of LT, the other party to sharing the Joint. Whilst their attitude was certainly based of eliminating steam haulage of their own trains beyond Rickmansworth, nevertheless it was in the positive context of reviving the pre-war 'New Works' scheme to electrify the Met to Amersham & Chesham. This was encouraged by the pressing need to replace their ageing multiple unit electric T stock and immediately after the war trials had been restarted with experimental cars with automatic doors that would be suitable for both Inner Circle and longer distance surface operation. Although some of the basic civil engineering work had been completed before the war, and some extra tracks added at Harrow North in 1948, much remained to be done and to speed matters in the early 1950's the original plans were revised to simplify some features.

The main changes were at Rickmansworth where the proposed 4-track layout was now reduced to 2 lines at Watford South Junction, thus avoiding the need to rebuild Rickmansworth station. In addition, the passing loop at Chorley Wood was omitted and it is interesting that the BR did not object to these changes which prevented any real reduction in this long-standing bottleneck. However a new bay platform was to be built at Chesham, which could enable the service frequency to be doubled, and more generous arrangements made at Amersham for the interchange with BR. Work began again in 1958 and moved steadily to completion in 1961 at a cost of £3.5M. The provision of two extra fast tracks from Harrow North to Watford Junction South, building a major new bridge at Northwood and constructing new stations, whilst maintaining an intensive train service was a noteworthy achievement. But there were delays in the delivery of the new A60 aluminium multiple electric stock from Cravens and so some steam hauled services also had to continue until some A60's were available. The last steam headed Chesham 'Shuttle' ran early on 12th September 1960. The new electrified public service started later that morning, mainly with the old T stock and with fast Chesham trains of venerable Dreadnought coaches hauled by the remaining Met Bo-Bo electric locos. This was to last until enough A60's were available in the autumn of 1961, but 4-tracking was not finished until June 1962.

The power struggles at BR that had led to the LMR taking responsibility for the Marylebone services took a stranger twist when in 1961 the line beyond Amersham was transferred from LT to the authority of the Western Region of BR. The only glimmer amidst the gloom of the continuing rundown of the Aylesbury line was the introduction in June of the first of the new Derby-built class 115 diesel multiple units which replaced the dwindling steam services in 1962. A few steam trains called at Quainton Road until 4th March 1965 and the odd DMU then ventured north of Aylesbury to Nottingham, but by the end of the year all remaining freight & passenger traffic had been switched to other routes and the Ministry of Transport approved closure of the original GC London Extension on 4th September 1966. The old Joint line now ended at Aylesbury.

Worse was to follow as the use of the remaining coal and oil concentration depots at Aylesbury , Marylebone and elsewhere declined. This together with the what were claimed as growing losses on their passenger services on the Joint were seized upon by BR and incorporated in yet another 5 year review to justify not investing further in the line. The consequence was the notorious proposal to close Marylebone and sell the site, whilst diverting their trains into Paddington station. In addition, the line from Amersham to Aylesbury would be singled and electrified under the responsibility of LTE. In a parallel move in 1983, BR announced a study to convert the old GW&GC Joint line into a high speed bus route. By 1984 this plan was supported by Sir Peter Parker, Chairman of BR, and coincided with the appearance of the notices announcing the intention to close Marylebone. As might be expected the reaction of commuters and the media was volcanic, leading to the local authorities taking the matter to Court. Although BR's decision was upheld by the Court, their failure to reveal the true economic justification for the closure – if one existed – gave the objectors a moral victory. As time dragged on with various inquiries it became apparent to the upper echelons of BR that their plans had been overtaken by events which now predicted a substantial growth in passengers using the Marylebone services. This arose from commuter growth in the catchment area plus the extra numbers generated by a series of LTE enlightened new fare schemes, such as the forerunner to the Travelcard. Together with the effects of the first proposals for the Heathrow Express, it became obvious to the operational managers that neither Paddington nor Baker Street would have sufficient capacity for all these extra services, and so BR did a U-turn and on the 30th April 1986 Marylebone was reprieved.

A smaller, but significant, about face was made by LT in relation to the Chesham branch which they clearly regarded as a nuisance. The first sign of trouble was in 1980 when LT became concerned over the viability of the line and this escalated when the two original bridges over the River Chess near Chesham became unsafe and needed to be replaced at a cost of £1.2 M. The local authorities refused to help and, somewhat ironically, proposed to close the end of the branch and build a new station on the site first selected by Watkin at the Moor. Fortunately the GLC Residuary Body took pity on the commuters and, as one of its last acts, funded the rebuilding of the bridges in 1986. Perhaps out of gratitude for this and certainly in remembrance for the long-awaited coming of the railway in 1889, the town convinced LT, railway enthusiasts and others that this centenary should be celebrated in style. The outcome in July 1989 was two weekends of steam operation between Chesham and Watford involving the preserved Met no1 E class 0-4-4T engine that had originally worked on the Joint. This engine had been restored to working order (along with much other important railway material) at what is now the flourishing Buckinghamshire Railway Centre located at Quainton Road. The popularity of the Chesham specials led to the series of 'Steam on the Met' events centred on Amersham which became outstanding demonstrations of professional collaboration between owners of a wide range preserved engines, volunteers in LT and the operators of the present Joint to create a frequent steam service within an existing intensive schedule of Chiltern Railway and LT trains. In recent years the never to be forgotten highlight was the early morning parallel running of two steam trains between Harrow and Moor Park, but sadly the event in 2000 seems likely to be the last.

oooo000oooo

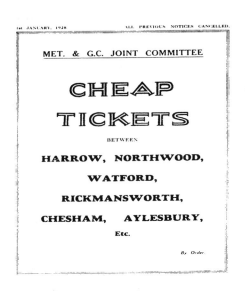

The Joint was only allowed to advertise trains within their area - two examples of 1928.

CHAPTER 11

TOWARDS PRIVATISATION

Following the reprieve to the expected closure of Marylebone station in 1986 the maintenance that had been deferred caused a complete review of the services on both the Aylesbury and High Wycombe lines. This gave an encouraging outcome and as result their revitalisation became a flagship project for the newly-formed Network South East established by the BR Chairman, Sir Bob Reid. Becoming the Thames & Chiltern Division, under the direction of entrepreneurial Chris Green, it produced an aggressive yet viable proposal for the regeneration of these services, the core of which was the renovation of Marylebone station itself, partly funded by an associated commercial property development on land on the west side originally bought by the GCR for expansion. The very old track was to be re-laid to provide a smoother and faster ride for the modern rolling stock that would replace the existing ageing Class 115 DMU's. With the whole system to be re-signalled and managed by an integrated electronic control centre at Marylebone, it incorporated a major advance in the piloting of a new Automatic Train Protection system. In the light of current concerns relating to rail safety it is very encouraging to know that this system has been fully deployed by this railway and that it works effectively and reliably.

The plan was completed in 1992 with the delivery of new lightweight Class 165 Network Turbo trains built by BR Engineering at York (11x3 and 28x2 cars) to a modern user–friendly design, which although limited to 75 mph, this was combined with good acceleration so that the schedules were substantially improved on both routes. To service this fleet a £4 M new maintenance facility was constructed in 1991 at Aylesbury and by the end of this phase some £65 M had been invested in the Chiltern Line. At the same time the northern end of the old GWR line at Snow Hill station was reinstated and this soon led to the popular introduction of a Chiltern Turbo service to Birmingham. To many this brought back memories of the intense competition between the GWR and LMS routes for the Birmingham traffic.

This coincided with the Thatcher Government thrust towards privatisation of the railways in the UK. Although consideration was first given to returning to the pre-war structure of the 'big four' railway companies a more radical solution was selected which could foster competition at all levels. The result was some 25 Train Operating Companies who pay for access to the rail network provided by

Railtrack. Both are supported by a host of private companies often derived from previous BR activities, which compete for maintenance, track work, catering etc. Inevitably this created complex relationships of responsibility and ownership that appeared would be even worse if applied to LT's specialised network, so it was decided to exclude them from the privatisation legislation at this stage.

In preparation for privatisation the passenger services of BR had already been separated into the 25 Train Operating Units, of which one was to be Chiltern Railways. This franchise was put out to competitive tender in 1996 and was awarded to management team led by the Managing Director, Adrian Shooter, backed by John Laing with 3i, with a 7 year franchise from 21st July 1996. Inevitably much of the expansion of Chiltern Railways has taken place on their Birmingham service particularly with the enhanced Class 168 DMU's from Adtranz. In common with many of the TOC's this stock was leased, in this case from Porterbrook Leasing in 1998. Such improved services have generated a steady overall growth in revenue from £14.5 M in 1994/5 to £33.5M in 1997/8. Like Railtrack and all the other TOC's, Chiltern Railways come under the influence of the Office of the Rail Regulator and the Strategic Rail Authority, with whom they have to agree performance targets. Recently the company has been restructured as M40 Trains with John Laing becoming the majority shareholder and is now embarking on the early re-negotiation of their franchise, due to expire in 2003.

The interest in privatising LT never went away and the management has been quite clear that their organisation had to evolve in a way that made this feasible. For example, the operation of the Metropolitan & Circle sub-surface lines are now a separate unit under a Managing Director of the InfraCo. Whilst the Labour Party were in opposition they argued against privatisation but when coming to power in1997 they recognised that some form of private finance would be necessary. Particularly in order to provide the capital required to eliminate the major arrears in maintenance and expand the system to cope with the demands of the growing population of London.

Turning now to the practical arrangements of sharing the old Joint between Chiltern Railways and the Metropolitan line of LT(Met), inevitably they retain some of the complexity of the old days. The infrastructure company, Railtrack, provides the track and signalling for Chiltern from Marylebone to Harrow South, from which point their trains share the 'fast' Met lines to Amersham, before reverting again to the Railtrack lines to Aylesbury (and occasionally beyond). Interestingly, there is an anomalous situation whereby the only significant lengths of un-electrified track that LT owns are at either end of the joint line: Harrow South and Amersham to Mantles Wood. In contrast to the homogenous BR era, the break up into the autonomous Chiltern Railways and the Met has necessitated the establishment of formal agreements in commercial and operational matters in a customer-contractor relationship to share the same line. In some way this turns the

In 1941 the existing Chesham branch train was replaced by an LNER C13 plus Met Ashbury coaches from the strategic reserve, to form an auto train. This saved the loco from running round the train at the end of each trip. In 1956 the 'Shuttle', with no.67416, climbs out from the Chess Valley heading for Chalfont. *(L V Reason)*

The other titled train in 1956 was the 'South Yorkshireman' and here A3 no.60111 heads the 5.15pm to Bradford on the 25th May through Moor Park. The photo was taken from the rickety wooden footbridge that matched the rest of the station and on the right are the pre-war preparations for adding fast tracks and electrification. *(L V Reason)*

On the local trains the LNER Thompson L1 tanks were now deposed by a succession of BR 2-6-4 types. Passing Chorley Wood Common, a freshly painted Brighton-built BR class 4 tank no.80143 heads an up Met train for the changeover to electric haulage at Rickmansworth. *(Stephen Gradidge)*

The traditional pick-up goods continued to operate until 1966. However the condition of the steam power steadily deteriorated and this photo shows a dirty Doncaster designed BR class 4 2-6-0 no.76040 negotiating the yard to the north of Rickmansworth. Eventually some were operated by class 24 Bo-Bo diesels. *(Stephen Gradidge)*

By 1960 some ex-LMS Stanier 2 cylinder class 4 2-6-4 tanks had taken over the local trains beyond Rickmansworth. Pictured from the footbridge by the Met goods shed at Rickmansworth are No.42629 and another with an illegible number, running forward to wait in the siding for their next turns. *(Stephen Gradidge)*

Rebuilding Moor Park station in 1960 for the delayed New Works scheme. The old wooden down platform is in the background and the new island platform for fast trains is in temporary use. The extra tracks were laid on the down side of the existing stations, except for Northwood which was constructed on the up side. *(NMR)*

BR class 2 Ivatt 2-6-2T's took over from the LNER C13's on the Chesham Shuttle just before electrification. The last full day of steam operation was 11th September 1960 and this picture shows no.41284 leaving Chesham carrying the traditional laurel wreath. As well as electrification a bay platform was added, but soon removed! *(Ron White)*

Similarly, at Rickmansworth the ritual of the changeover between steam and electric power took place for the last time. Whilst standing astride the centre conductor, the stationman holds the vacuum pipe of the Met coach as the ex-LMS 2-6-4T no.42066 moves forward. One doubts if this would now be allowed by the HSE! *(F C le Maquais)*

Ironically, by the 1960's the only consolation for the reduction in long distance services over the Joint was the increase in the different types of motive power. Diesel traction began to appear on some freight trains and here a EE class 40 no.D217 is pulling an up goods/parcels out of the Rickmansworth curve bound for Marylebone yard. *(S Gradidge)*

Double-heading was often employed as a convenient method of transferring a light engine. At the new Moor Park LT station in 1960, before the recently ballasted extra tracks had been electrified, an up 'Ord' passes with an ex-LNER Thompson class B1 4-6-0 no.61078 built in 1942, piloting a Britannia 4-6-2. *(Stephen Gradidge)*

The main engineering project to implement the pre-war LT electrification scheme from Harrow to Amersham was the skew bridge at Northwood over the Rickmansworth Road. This 1961 picture shows one of the first A60 aluminium multiple electric stock on a down train crossing the new bridge, whilst the extra tracks are completed. *(LT)*

In parallel with the LT electrification to Amersham, BR introduced Type 115 diesel multiple units to replace the local steam services from Marylebone to Aylesbury. Here at Amersham in 1962, the down A60 8-car set has terminated and the new station layout allows passengers to cross to the DMU to continue on to Aylesbury. *(LT)*

clock back to the days of the Joint and regular liaison meetings are held between them to discuss such matters as timetabling, special working i.e. engineering occupation, leaf fall, commercial issues, safety cases etc. Formally the shared lines from Harrow South to Mantles Wood at Amersham are under the direction of the Met via their Control Centre at Baker Street and through the signal boxes at Harrow, Rickmansworth and Amersham. In this section the Met can manage the train movements and keep in voice contact by radio with drivers of both the companies. All Chiltern trains are fitted with the standard LT tripcocks so that they conform to their signalling in preventing overrunning signals at danger. These tripcocks are tested automatically as each train leaves Amersham station. In managing the passage of the trains of the two companies, allowance has to be made for their different characteristics i.e the Chiltern trains have a higher acceleration and are somewhat lighter, which can affect 'leaf fall' performance.

A Chiltern Railways train is allowed to enter the Joint providing it is within 3 mins of its timetabled path, if not it is held to the next available slot. On the other hand if the Chiltern train is on time and yet held up by the Met, then it receives financial compensation in relation to the time of the delay. Inevitably the characteristics of the two services are quite different i.e. the Met runs a higher density service for whom 30 secs is a long time, it is affected by the congestion at the Met/Inner Circle junction at Baker Street and the vagaries of a service starting from the City. Whereas, Chiltern seek to be a faster longer distance line and thus desire to see Rickmansworth station radically changed so that the current speed restriction of 25mph could be raised to their average speed of 60mph. For them time is also important but 30 secs is a time that it is possible to retrieve by high acceleration. The only minor point of conflicting movement between Chiltern trains is where the Birmingham and Aylesbury lines merge at Neasden.

From the commercial aspect, Chiltern Railways pay access charges to Railtrack for their own lines and also to the Met for using the Joint. Although the passenger ticket revenue originating between Amersham and Harrow is shared, it raises some of the perennial difficulties of determining which route the passengers took when they have the option of using either service between Harrow and London. Currently a manual sample check is made twice a year in order to agree the split in the revenue, but soon both routes will be fully equipped with automatic ticket barriers and it will then be possible to obtain an accurate division of receipts. In spite of the necessity for such formal agreements between the Chiltern and the Met, there is certainly a spirit of 'give and take' between them and when there is an operational problem to try to ensure that passengers do not suffer. Compared to the old Joint, now the atmosphere is completely different in that whilst both are rightly independent with their own objectives, there is also the recognition that they have to work together and that there are positive benefits to be achieved by sharing success.

ooooo000ooooo

CHAPTER 12

INTO THE NEW MILLENNIUM

The immediate concerns of the Met and Chiltern Railways arise from the financial and operational aspects of maintaining the current services and coping with increasing peak demand. In the case of the Met the problems relate to the continuing bottleneck at Baker Street and the inevitable need to soon replace the poor-riding A60 stock which was built in 1961 and refurbished in 1994. Whereas in the case of Chiltern Railways the popularity of the Aylesbury service and the growth in their 'heartland' in the Midlands around Leamington Spa (a new Warwick Parkway will open 2001) are stretching the capacity of their fleet of DMU's. But over both of them the lack of cohesion in the present Government's transport policy is creating some clouds of uncertainty.

The intention is to get the private sector to assist in funding the refurbishment of the London Transport Rail system that is so obviously needed. This is likely to be via a Private-Public–Partnership scheme and it was expected that Railtrack would be the preferred bidder for an 'InfraCo' contract to take responsibility for the track, signalling & stations of all sub-surface lines of LT, but this will now be put out to open tender. Somewhat impracticably, the Government hopes that this will somehow allow mainline trains to interconnect via the Inner Circle. Meanwhile an 'OpsCo' will run the LT train operations. Of course Chiltern Railways are already in the private sector as a 'TransCo' with an infrastructure largely provided by Railtrack and therefore if the proposals for LT take place, then all the infrastructure of the Joint could be the responsibility of Railtrack. However the main uncertainty for Chiltern Railways is the question of negotiating an extension their franchise from 2003 to enable major investment to take place. Nevertheless their new owners John Laing (M40 Trains) have vigorous plans for the future and should be well-placed to retain the franchise. These are mainly directed at major improvements to their Marylebone –Birmingham route, a follow-on order for more 168's (from Adtranz,, improved and styled as 170 Turbostars), passing loops at Beaconsfield, completion of doubling the track at Bicester and the re-opening of Moor Street station at Birmingham. But this will also have consequences for the Joint with refurbishment of the present class 165's and the need to expand their maintenance facilities at Aylesbury, or elsewhere. Interestingly, in an echo from the Watkin era, it is also intended to examine the possibility of creating the long-mooted West Hampstead interchange linking the Chiltern with the Midland mainline, North London Line and the Met & Jubilee Lines.

Turning to new railways, an obvious missing link since the construction of the Watford branch by the Joint has been a connection from Croxley Green to the nearby branch of the then LMSR. Joining the Croxley stations by a relatively short line would have been much easier before the land became developed. But even now the difficulties of a flyover would be counterbalanced by providing a direct route for the Met to the actual centre of Watford – rather than their present station at Cassiobury Park. In addition such a link would give the West Coast mainline an alternative approach into London, if only for football specials bound for Wembley. In recent years formal plans have been put forward for a 'Croxley Rail Link' and although there would be practical problems to be overcome, such as the compatibility of the electric power supplies and safety issues, the main question as usual is – who pays? This year the Herts CC , Three Rivers DC and Watford Council joined with Railtrack and LUL to support the proposal with £5M and with an estimated £12.5M from fares: the Government is being asked to fund the remaining £30.5M.

From a chronological viewpoint the next scheme dates back to the closure of the GCR mainline and the subsequent increase in road congestion which led to proposals in the 1960's to turn the old trackbed into a roadway to London. With the revitalisation by Chiltern Railways these proposals faded away but in the past two years they have been reborn in the shape of the 'Central Railway Company' scheme. The scale of this project would have pleased Sir Edward Watkin, in that it envisages a 250 mile rail link from Liverpool to the Channel Tunnel and thus to the Continent, at a cost of £3.7Bn. It is expected to generate £1.3 Bn of revenue within two years and grow at a rate of 5% pa. The railway would carry lorries and for 80% of the route utilise existing track such as the old GCR mainline. The proposals still seem nebulous and do not address the practicalities of achieving the necessary loading gauge or crossing London, but they have unleashed a storm of protest from the residents in Bucks who could well be affected by inconvenience and planning 'blight'. Nevertheless the company has received some vague Government support and is currently lobbying Parliament, the City and the Strategic Rail Authority.

In contrast to other nations the UK seems to find it difficult to make such political/financial decisions on large infrastructure projects and this is well demonstrated by the 'Crossrail' project. Launched with fanfares by Lord Parkinson in 1990 it was intended to ease London's East-West traffic problems by a new connection near Acton to the present Extension line (from Aylesbury & Chesham) via Neasden, and to the 'Western' from Reading. Then from Acton to Paddington on present lines and so under London by a new deep-level 6m dia. tunnel with major intermediate stations to Liverpool Street and thence on the existing route to Shenfield. Crossrail trains would replace both the present

Chiltern services and also those of the Met to Amersham/Chesham. These services would be provided by 12 car (25kv overhead powered) stock with a capacity of 1800 passengers. The existing Watford & Uxbridge Met trains would continue to run to Baker Street and the Chiltern Birmingham ones to Marylebone. But as time passed Government interest waned and the estimated cost of the line, which would require substantial civil engineering works for tunnelling, lengthening platforms and improving clearances for overhead electrification, escalated to over £8Bn. During this period a LT team of 200 staff tasked with planning the project had produced some 15,000 drawings, the requisite procurement specifications and a design for the new rolling stock (type 341's). However by 1996 the scheme was put on a 'care and maintenance' basis after expenditure of £144M and is now orientated to protect the access to intended route. Recently, possibly spurred by the impending reorganisation of London, the City of London and others revived the core of the proposal consisting of the new deep tunnel from Paddington to Liverpool Street at a cost of £2.8Bn. In response the Government made it clear the any decision on this would lie with the incoming new Mayor of London, which raises questions over their support for those parts in the home counties.

The most recent initiative has been the attempt in 1999 to revive the old LMSR cross-country railway line running from Oxford via Bicester, the erstwhile Claydon (LNER) & Verney (Met) Junctions, Bletchley, Bedford and Sandy. It was on this line before the last war that the Oxford and the Cambridge Railway Societies held their annual dinner on a train between the two cities! At an estimated cost of some £237M this "East-West Rail Link" would connect the ports of Felixstowe & Harwich to Swindon thus providing a much needed relief route for freight around London. Unfortunately the Sandy–Bedford section would need to be re-laid and there is the complication of some houses having recently been built on the old track bed. However if it does materialise, it will have interesting consequences for the Extension.

Indeed all the schemes just outlined could dramatically change the nature of the existing Joint, but in order to make progress they all seem to need a degree of governmental and financial commitment to improve the railway infrastructure in this country that to date has been sadly lacking. Therefore the shape of the Extension is likely to maintain the status quo but the division of responsibility is likely to change under the PPP initiatives and the policy of the incoming Mayor of London, Ken Livingstone, whose remit will extend as far as Northwood. However, the current re-evaluation of the fundamental organisation of the UK railway system following on from the recent tragic Clapham, Watford, Southall and Paddington disasters could well bring about a completely new regime. But whatever happens it is likely to involve, in some way, the sharing of the Extension well into the next century plus the spirit of the old Joint to make it work in practice.

ooooOOOoooo

APPENDIX 1

THE JOINT FROM THE MINUTE BOOKS

The Minutes were not only bound in the original hand written form but were also printed until the mid-1930's, from when only a typewritten record was kept. The majority of the content of these books is taken up with minutiae and repetitious items from changes in wages to winners of the garden competitions. This is therefore a selection of the most significant, interesting and curious pieces that, apart from detailing the activities of the Joint, also provide a facet of social history.

1906

Some meetings of both the Joint Committee and the Officers Conference were held before the Joint formally came into existence on the 2nd April 1906, probably in order to establish some of the interpretations of the Agreement so that it would come into operation smoothly. The first meeting was an Officers Conference held on the 8th February with the GCR team of H Bowden, W Clow, J Lees, W Robinson, C Smith & G Warburton led by R Haigh Brown (Superintendent), whilst H B Palmer (Met Superintendent of the Line) fielded W Brown, F Crocker & J Finlayson. No Chairman or Secretary were recorded but at a subsequent meeting Haigh Brown took the Chair and thereafter alternated with Palmer. The following matters were agreed:

-Currently all the staff comes from the Met and now the GCR will fill all vacancies until each grade has an equal number from each company. The appointment of stationmasters is subject to the agreement of both. This excludes Aylesbury station that is joint with the GWR.

-In disciplinary cases the Management Company can act without reference to the other, when it requires urgent action as in the instance of drunkenness.

-The GCR urges the Met to adopt its practice whereby the Superintendent of the Line controls all goods staff.

-Facilities will be provided for the GCR to stable stock at Aylesbury and trials will be performed for stabling and run-round at Chesham, Rickmansworth and Great Missenden.

-GCR to provide a steam railcar for the Aylesbury – Verney Junction service.

-Met complaint that goods were being routed from Chesham by the 8.10 to Marylebone and thence by the GW & GC Joint line (to the advantage of the GCR) rather than via Quainton Road.

-Cheap tickets were agreed for 'medical staff, patients & friends' at Mount Vernon Hospital.

-A long discussion on the division of receipts on season tickets between Harrow & London that was referred to Fay and Selbie for resolution. This was not settled until 1913, when Fay finally agreed to a Met 55% & GCR 45% split when Selbie accepted that *"the liability for accidents with shunting engines only relates to those provided by the Joint"*.

-Discussion on supply of uniforms to staff:

No. of Men	181	
No. of Overcoats	103	Every 2 years
No. of Dresscoats	20	Every year
No. of Jackets	139	Every year
No. of Vests	139	Every year
No. of Pairs of Trousers	159	Every 6 months (serge in winter, tweed in summer)
No. of Caps	181	Every year
No. of pairs of Boots	148	Every 6 months

This is the only direct reference to the total number of Joint staff as the returns in the Minutes just give the changes i.e. number of retirements, promotions etc.

The first real Joint Committee Meeting was held on 8th March with Sir Charles Mclaren(Met and later Lord Aberconway) in the Chair plus Sir W Birt & Col. J Mellor and Selbie as the Secretary. The GCR were represented by Sir Alexander Henderson, E Chapman & W Viccars. Those in attendance were (Met): Ellis, Kitat, & Seaton with (GCR); Fay, Holt, Davies & Rowlandson, This meeting of the leading players started with the approval of the recommendations given the earlier Officers Conference and then a number of basic matters were decided:

-Remuneration of Committee members to be £100 pa. *As some were on several other joint boards such payments could be significant.*

-A separate account to be opened for the Joint at the Met's bankers.

-Track maintenance to be split with GCR to the north of milepost 28½ (near Great Missenden) and Met to the south.

-Locomotive power charges to be 7/- per hour.

-Plans approved for a new interchange station at Willesden Green at a cost of £7,000 but final decision deferred to the Chairmen of the Companies.

-Noted a petition of the people of Watford requesting a 'branch line' to their town but only agreed to prepare the necessary Bill.

-Agreed to modify the track layout at Aylesbury *(site of the crash in 1904)* but as the GWR did not concur, Fay and Selbie would discuss the matter with them.

1907

Joint Committee

-GWR approves the new track layout at Aylesbury but refuses to contribute to the cost of £5,000.

-Harrow South to be a Joint signal box with the signalmen appointed on an 'alternate' basis

-All iron bridges to be replaced by steel ones.

-Subscription of 1 guinea to the Aylesbury Fire Brigade. *This was the forerunner of a number of annual donations to local charities.*

Officers Conference

-GCR unwilling to change the times of their trains as it upset their overall timetabling.

1908

Joint Committee

-Agreed to issue own Joint Rule Book based on that of the Railway Clearing House. *There were only minor additions and these were shown in bold print.*

-Approved improving access at Chorley Wood. *These cases continued over the years as access was needed on the opposite side to the station buildings and motor cars became common.*

-Track replacement agreed at 2 miles pa.

-The Joint Committee strongly urged Fay and Selbie to settle outstanding differences or bring in an arbitrator.

Officers Conference

-Retain those staff over 60 yrs old, if in satisfactory health.

-Anthony de Rothschild to pay for a telephone to be installed at Waddesdon stn.

-Met wanted to employ their man as the Line Inspector for the Joint, but GCR said that it should 'alternate'.

1909

Joint Committee

-The proposal by a Golf Club syndicate for a halt at Sandy Lodge was accepted, if they would guarantee traffic of over £350 pa.

-Fires at Chenies Estate, near Chalfont Road station, caused by sparks from engines. The Duke of Bedford offered to cut down the undergrowth for £3-4 pa.

-Court case over bull killed on the line at Aylesbury in 1907.

Officers Conference *(W Holt becomes Traffic Superintendent of the Met)*

-Proposal to extend sidings at stations Rickmansworth to Amersham due to growth in traffic.

1910

Joint Committee

-Sandy Lodge halt, building agreed at £555.

-Staff allowed to join Met Pension Fund or GC & Joint Lines Friendly Society as appropriate.

-Land let on down side of Northwood station for Bessborough Dairies for "model cowshed & dairy with ornamental tea rooms".

- Agreed that Conciliation Board awards be given to staff.

Officers Conference *(W Clow becomes Line Superintendent of the GCR)*

-Plans for improved signalling agreed.

-Review of rental properties (16 such generated £107 pa) and leases, including Chesham watercress beds.

-Telephone installed at Harrow *and gradually across the Joint, e.g. Chesham in 1912.*
-Wage bill increases by £1 per week.

1911

Joint Committee

-Aylesbury UDC presses for footbridge at Court Close to replace dangerous crossing.

-Secretarial work by the Met charged at £900 pa.

-Fourteen fire claims for £135, offered £59 in settlement.

-Lord Ebury offers his land for sidings at Sandy Lodge halt.

-Confidential: Proposal for the new branch to Watford discussed at length. Agreed to seek powers via own Bill and that these should be vested in the Joint.

Officers Conference

-*Gas v electric lighting is an ongoing issue.* Gas for Chesham accepted on costs.

1912

Joint Committee

-Report of Chesham 'Shuttle' running into the buffers at Chalfont Road on 21/12/12 causing considerable damage to rolling stock & track. Only one passenger was in the train, a Mr Towns, and his claim for injury had been disposed of by a payment of £10 compensation plus 12/6d for medical fees.

-LNWR objects to proposed Joint Watford branch and it was agreed to raise the height of the line so that the LNWR could pass underneath if necessary.

-Request from Rickmansworth Gravel Co. for relaying of their sidings as a result of the proposed branch to Watford.

-Royal assent on 7/8/12 to Watford branch Bill.

Officers Conference

-Depot established at Aylesbury South Yard for cleaning cattle wagons at £150.

-Provision for a shelter at Chalfont Road (£40) in response to vociferous complaints in inclement weather by 'Shuttle' passengers.

1913

Joint Committee

-Water for locos at Aylesbury has to be pumped from a stream by a GW engine at a cost of £124 pw so it was agreed to replace this by a gas engine (£40).

-Bill prepared for Halt at North Harrow.

-Agreed to relay 2miles 908 yds of track in the next year.

-Purchase authorised of a travelling crane (Cowans & Sheldon £575) and a match truck (GCR £153). *The only item of Joint stock.*

Officers Conference

-Pay increases from Conciliation Board giving an overall rise in the wage bill of the 142 staff of £10-5-8d per week. But 'consolidation' of existing bonuses reduced this to £5-6-9d.

-Store for foot warmers at Chesham to be used for watercress hampers (£3).

-Signalling delays due to signal spacing and operation of electric locking mechanisms to be rectified (£746).

1914 Outbreak of First War
Joint Committee

-Hold put on construction of Watford branch due to war but land continued to be purchased, including 37 acres at £490 per acre from Gonville & Caius College.

-Regarding Watford branch, a claim was received from builders Froude, Dawson & Hunt for £15,570 for the 'annihilation' of one of their businesses on 3 ½ acres by the canal. Enquiries revealed that only one set of accounts existed for their two activities and that the other book had been destroyed in a fire, just before a new partner joined the firm.*(!)* The case went to arbitration and was settled at £3,500.

-Proposal to single track between Quainton Road and Verney Junction.

-North Harrow Halt to be built by own labour to minimise cost.

1915
Joint Committee

-War bonus paid of 2-3s pw.

-Complaints over poor condition of Joint cottages at California, near Aylesbury station, without flushing toilets or running water and with bad drainage, damp and leaky roofs.

Officers Conference

-Water column on Rickmansworth up platform to be moved to the end of it because trains with more than 5 coaches have to back-up to take water. (£40)

-Agreed to build a ticket hut at Wendover station for the use of soldiers from the nearby camp as their numbers are causing congestion in the booking office.

-LNWR ceasing cartage from Chesham to their station at Berkhamsted. Agreed therefore new clerk, porter & lad porter for Chesham to deal with extra work.

-List of Joint staff included who have joined the colours.

-Accidents: A Mr Toop, travelling on the 1pm train from Marylebone noticed that a lady in his compartment wished to alight at North Harrow, but was unable to open the door. Mr Toop tried to assist, opened the door by leaning out of the window and got out to assist the lady to alight. However the train started and both fell to the platform. After helping the lady up he made a rush for the moving train and slipped off the foot-board upon the track, sustaining a slight injury. Agreed, an expression of sympathy to Mr Toop and the sum of £5.

-At Aylesbury on 5/3/15 a horse and cart crossing the north end of the platform were hit by a motor-train, which demolished the cart. The Committee considered their foreman to be at fault and settled the claim of £51-13-6d for £28-3-0d.

-Parcel cartage agents appointed for Amersham. *The review of these appointments was a routine item.*

-Mishaps & compensation: *Consideration of these claims was a regular item.*

C. Lovelock	shunter	foot crushed & amputated	£38-17-9d
		artificial limb	£11- 5-6d
J. Pratt	ganger	fatal	£274-12-0d
W. Carter	porter	ankle sprain	£5-13-4d
H. Marks	porter	scalp wound	£5-10-6d

-Pay for Stationmasters agreed for Aylesbury Joint & for Harrow at £180 pa with £70 pa (including a house) for Grandborough Road.

1916

Joint Committee

-Noted that 5¼ miles of track need replacement in the GCR section and 10 miles in Met section. The Ministry of Munitions would be approached urgently to release the necessary materials.

-Pinner Wesleyan Chapel bought for £250 for future widening of line.

-Revised agreement over sharing Aylesbury station with GW & GC Joint Cttee.

-A troublesome case of a Mr Greves, in relation to obtaining some of his land for the Watford Extension. This was settled by agreeing to build an ornamental bridge for access to Cassio Bridge House.

Officers Conference

-Met having difficulty of starting to supply uniforms and GCR agreed to provide until the end of 1916.

-Family excursion trips to visit troops at Halton Camp were cancelled due to lack of bookings.

1917

-G Turner, pay increased from 6d to 9d per wagon for cleaning cattle wagons, 'for the period of the war'.

1918 End of First War

Joint Committee

-Agreed to sales of timber. Chesham Vale: 6359 cu.ft. for £350 and from Watford Extension land some 10,000 cu.ft. for £1045.

-13 staff still on active service.

-Agreed to provision of overcoats to Fogmen at each 'fogging point'.

1919

-More land bought at Aylesbury and some existing land sold for council housing.

-Further land obtained for Watford Extension.

-Ongoing debates about electric v gas lighting.

1920

-Junction telephone line agreed between Baker St. & Marylebone stations (£20).

-Watford Extension Act powers extended.

-Dispense with Quainton Road Junction signalbox and extend double track into the station giving a saving of £520 pa.

1921

-Agreement on painting Joint stations for £5,611.

-Due to depressed economic circumstances staff reduced by 11 uniform & 7 clerical grades and all over 60's retired.

1922

Joint Committee

-Fay & Selbie to apply to the Treasury to guarantee the interest on the capital expenditure on the Watford Extension. *(Unsuccessful)*

-Signal boxes at Pinner, Northwood, Chorley Wood, Amersham & Stoke Mandeville to be closed and switched out on Sundays thus saving £28 pw.

The late delivery of the new aluminium multiple electric A stock resulted in the use of the old T stock and Bo-Bo locos over the Extension until 1961. As the evening fast Chesham hauled by no.18 'Oliver Goldsmith' enters Chorley Wood, a sub-station has been built but the original Met signal box and goods yard remain. *(Stephen Gradidge)*

Around 1963 a BR class 7P6F Britannia 4-6-2 no.70049 passes through Chorley Wood with an express in the early morning. By now LMR had taken over responsibility from Eastern Region of BR for Marylebone and a run down of longer distance passenger and goods services followed as a prelude to expected closure. *(Stephen Gradidge)*

Chorley Wood is reputed to be the coldest place in the Chilterns and in 1963 the 08.15 Nottingham - Marylebone semi-fast train passes through an the remains of an overnight snowfall. No.45238 is in charge, one of several grimy ex-LMS class 5 4-6-0's now relegated to the Joint. *(Stephen Gradidge)*

A year later and more snow on the Joint, this time the scene is Rickmansworth with an up ex-Nottingham semi-fast emerging from the speed restriction on the curve, hauled by ex-LMS Royal Scot class 4-6-0 no.46163. Sometimes these worked the pick-up goods and one ignored the weight limit and ended up at Chesham by mistake! *(S Gradidge)*

The local services from Marylebone had been improved in 1961 with the introduction of DMU's. But under LMR the decline of the longer distance train services accelerated. This is a typical example, with a morning ex Nottingham train at Harrow at 11.11am headed by a class 5 no.45114. The last such train ran on 3rd Sept 1966. *(Bill Piggott)*

The last steam service trains on the Joint were the LT engineering movements hauled by their ex-GWR 0-6-0 pannier tanks. This picture shows no.L94 (ex-7752), which was later withdrawn with their other remaining pannier in 1971, heading the Met steam crane south through Rickmansworth back to Neasden Depot. *(Stephen Gradidge)*

In 1988 Chris Green of BR formed the Thames & Chiltern Division which later revamped the existing DMU services with the introduction of the Chiltern Line with new type 165 turbo diesels. To maintain this new fleet a £4M modern large maintenance facility was constructed just north of Aylesbury in 1991. *(Clive Foxell)*

Although it never happened during the Joint era, the parallel running of two steam trains on the LT four-track section was a highlight of the recent 'Steam on the Met' events. Making an impressive start from Harrow in 1996 are two ex-GW engines, pannier no.9446 and mogul no.7325. They will diverge after Moor Park. *(Ron Potter)*

-All land had been procured for the Watford Extension at a cost of £51,908 and although there had been some doubt on the need for a northern junction to Rickmansworth this was agreed, together with the additional sidings for a 'shuttle' train. The lowest tender at £149,874 from Messrs Logan & Hemmingway, offering completion in 21 months, was accepted.

-Bookstall contracts were placed with W H Smith & Son requiring 12½% of gross sales, 65% of advertising revenue and a rent of £2,000 plus rates pa.

Officers Conference

-Accident: In Halton Camp siding a Joint shunter moved 7 loaded wagons without seeing that the driver of the Halton Camp loco had sent his fireman down beneath his engine to clear clinker from the grate. Unfortunately the fireman was badly injured as the wagons hit the engine and was awarded compensation of £210 plus a weekly allowance.

- These were the last meetings attended by Sir Sam Fay before his retirement.

1923 With the grouping of the mainline railways the LNER absorbed the GCR. The Joint administration continued as before, only GCR representatives were gradually replaced by those from the LNER. Also the location of the "GCR" meetings was occasionally moved to Liverpool Street station.

-Government gave compensation of about £30,000 for 'wartime possession'.

-Track to be relayed in year: LNER = 1½ and Met = 2miles.

-Vending machine contract made with British Vending Automatic Co. at 17½% of gross revenue.

- Met wish to electrify Harrow to Rickmansworth and will perform all the work, but the LNER reserve the right to use the tracks and current for their own trains.

- Due to heavy traffic there was a need to introduce new automatic signalling and a burrowing junction for the Uxbridge line at Harrow. The cost of £77,000 would be split between the LNER and the Met.

-Aylesbury Joint station needed to be reconstructed and it was agreed that the cost of £48,444 would be split between the Met & GC and the GW & GC Joint Committees.

-Accident: Mr Jones's lorry was damaged at Amersham sidings when brought alongside a coal wagon, whose flap door was lowered so that when the train moved away the lorry was dragged along the tracks. It was regarded as the fault of Ewers, the porter, who was suspended for one day.

1924

-Delay of 8 months expected in finishing north curve of the Watford extension due to difficult conditions but 50% of contractor retention released. Agreed to build new station at Croxley Green with 6 cottages plus signal box at junction.

-Agreed improved milk handling facilities at Harrow (currently 87 churns/day) and Grandborough Road (50).

-Met breakdown van at Aylesbury, which was not taken over by the Joint, is in bad condition and will be scrapped. Met or LNER services will be used instead.

-Windmill water pump at Great Missenden to be replaced by a gas engine.

1925

-Siding proposed for Moor Park (£1,400).

-Public footpaths cross the lines at the County boundary and at mile post 14½.
Agreed that footbridges should replace these. (£450 plus £150 from Council)
-Extra siding for 8 wagons at Quainton Road.
-Watford to be opened for service on 2nd November and the extension will be administered by the Watford Joint (or Met & LNER Joint) Committee. These Committee meetings will follow the Met & GC Joint Committee meetings and members will be paid £50 pa.
-Aylesbury reconstruction completed (£38,755)
-Motor vans acquired by the Joint to replace carter agents will be serviced & painted by the LNER.
-Annual renewal of cab licences to operate from 'Joint' stations.
-Watford branch needs extra staff:-
Croxley Green = 7 inc. Mr Eldridge, stationmaster from Quainton Road.
Watford = 15 inc. Mr Springthorpe, stationmaster from Granborough Road.

1926 General Strike

-Loyalty bonus for those that remained on duty during the General Strike.
-Land sold for road widening at Chesham (Nashleigh Hill).
-Staff economies due to the depression with 'withdrawals' saving £10 pw.
-Cost of Watford Junction signal box split as follows:

Met & LNER Jt. Cttee.	21½ /27 ths.
Met & GC Jt. Ctte.	5 ½ /27 ths.
Rickmansworth Gravel Co.	14/129 ths. of above

-Purchase of AEC lorry for £750, to compete with the LMS for paper traffic.

1927

-Split in costs of new signal boxes:

	Harrow, North	Harrow, South	Quainton Road
Met & GC Jt.	11 8/9 /21 ths	42½ /52 ths	29/34 ths
Met	9 1/9 /21 ths	9½ /52 ths	
LNER			5/34 ths

-Two boys were killed on separate occasions whilst taking a short cut across the line at Court Close footpath near Aylesbury.
-National Benzole acquire tenancy at Chalfont and Latimer for a fuel depot.

1928

Joint Committee
-Stoke Mandeville signal box closed and operated from Aylesbury.
-North Harrow Halt made a station due to increase in receipts from £2,468 in 1922 to £15,078 in 1927.
-Land slip again at Moor Park.
-Agreement with unions for a 2½ % reduction in pay due to economic situation.
Officers Conference
-Seeing that retirees are now entitled to a state pension of 10/- pw, this will be deducted from their company pension.
-Agreed that a lock-up be provided at Aylesbury for storing fish overnight.

1929

Joint Committee

-Aylesbury Town council wishes to build a bridge at Close Court.

-Agent carter's are using horses which are not a credit to the Joint and thus the Co. will take over and improve the services by purchasing its own motor vehicles:

1 Thornycroft	30cwt lorry	= £486
1 Thornycroft	1 ton lorry	
1 Morris	1 ton lorry	= £241
4 Thornycroft	2 ton lorries	= £2,300

due to increasing business another order was later placed for another Thornycoft 4 ton lorry at £717.

-Extra siding agreed for Pinner due to goods traffic growing from 25,183 tons in 1913 to 49,568 in 1928.

Officers Conference

-Underman W Owen killed by a LNER express at Aylesbury: gratuity £25.

-Chesham station wins best garden competition. *(again)*

-Watford Committee to buy another lorry, a Thornycroft 30cwt van for £486.

1930

Joint Committee

-In the only record in these Minutes of a personal nature, it was noted that Robert Hope Selbie (General Manager of the Met) had died (whilst attending a confirmation service for his son at St. Paul's Cathedral). "He was regarded with the greatest esteem and the Committee felt a deep sense of loss".

-Accidents: Lady Taylor was alighting from a train at Moor Park with the assistance of her daughter, when the lad porter thought that she was boarding the train and signalled it to leave. Lady Taylor was thrown onto the platform sustaining serious injuries. She had claimed £250 and noting that there could be adverse comment against the Company, it was agreed to offer £200 subject to clearance by Sir Ralph Wedgwood Chairman of the LNER.

-Gangers Sweet, Underwood & Drury were caught in a squall of rain at Harrow and were hit by a train. Sweet (with 5 children) and Drury were killed and were awarded £600 & £508 respectively.

-Approved development of the Weller Estate at Amersham plus improvements to the station approach and footpath to the downside platform.

Officers Conference

-Proposal to convert from telegraphic to telephone communication system and reconfigure circuits to reduce congestion.

-Two gangers killed at N. Harrow Junction by an electric train in a rainstorm: gratuity £600 each.

-More staff economies.

-Damage by rats to Chesham goods shed.

-All existing automatic colour light signals to be given an illuminated letter A to show that a 'stop' may be passed at danger under the '1 minute rule'.

-Remove old wooden turntable at Aylesbury.

1931

-Pay reduced again by 5% for all staff and including the Committee,

-Agreed to purchase an additional 30 cwt Thornycroft lorry for £438.

-Platforms at Harrow, Pinner, Northwood, Moor Park & Rickmansworth to be lengthened due to growth in local passenger journeys between Watford - Rickmansworth & Harrow i.e. from 4M in 1922 to 7M in 1930.

1932

Joint Committee

-Met Rule Book to apply south of Rickmansworth and the LNER one north thereof.

-Agreed to build a new station at Northwood Hills at a cost of £12,000, of which the builders of the estate will contribute £6,000 and guarantee a growth in overall traffic receipts.

-Improve facilities at Moor Park station, which currently has no lavatories.

1933 Met absorbed by the LPTB on 1ˢᵗ July 1933, but this line remains under the Met & GC Joint Committee.

-LTPB was represented on the Joint Committee by Lord Ashfield, Sir J Gilbert & F Pick whilst the LNER team was initially led by Hon E Butler Henderson with W Gair. On the Officers Conference G Halley led for the Met and V Barrington-Ward for the LNER.

-Rule Books of LPTB & LNER adopted.

-LPTB to take over exclusive rights for commercial advertising, except the Joint station at Aylesbury, and 75% of the revenue to go to the Joint.

-Proposal to close Brill branch.

1934

-Approved the scheme to widen the lines between Harrow & Rickmansworth and now seek the necessary parliamentary powers.

-Further reduction in wages of 2½ %.

-Gave notice to the owners of the O&AT (Brill Branch), led by Earl Temple, to terminate the 'arrangement'. However the owners refused to accept the right of the Met to do this. Therefore agreed to allow the period of notice and then cease payments.

1935

Joint Committee

-Convert lorries from solid to pneumatic tyres in order to reduce licence duty.

-Widening Scheme: Encourage Middlesex C.C. to replace the existing Roxborough Road bridge at Harrow and press the Middx.C.C. and the Herts C.C. to replace the other relevant bridges. *They subsequently agreed to pay for 40% of this work.*

Officers Conference

-Several claims for grass fires caused by engines.

-Proposal to close line from Quainton Road to Verney Junction.

Loss of income = Met share of overall trips	£1269	
Those exclusive to the branch	£1027	
Total	£2296	

143

Savings =   Maintenance   £480
                  Staff   £1173
                  LNER/LPTB working expenses £685
                              Total £2338
Therefore annual saving on closure would be £42 and it was agreed to withdraw the service and close Winslow Road and Granborough Road. The demolition of these would cost £1706.

-Agreed closure of Brill branch on 1.12.1935

1936

-The Station Master at Chesham, F W Finch *(winner of many garden competitions)* to retire on a pension of £200/yr, split as his service i.e. Met 22yrs& 302 days, Joint 28yrs& 320 days.

-After complaints by local Councils about the state of Chalfont & Latimer, agreed to improvements at a cost of £2,254

-Maintenance of all road vehicles lorries to be transferred from the Joint to the LNER and two LNER lorries to be operated by the Joint at Harrow.

-Track works next year 'north' = 2m 522yds and 'south' = 15m 1244yds.

1937

-Passenger service withdrawn between Quainton Road & Verney Junction on 6th August 1936 and therefore the Joint will reduce its share of the costs with the LMS at Verney Junction.

-Brill branch has been surrendered to its owners and as the GWR had paid £100 to each partner to cross the branch they would pay Earl Temple (O&AT) the £200 plus interest.

-The LNER wishes to realign the track at Quainton Road in order to increase the speed limit to above 25 mph. It will pay any costs involved.

-Rebuilding the LTPB shed at Neasden depot means that it will be impractical to house their 29 Met steam engines. Thus Met steam power and freight will pass to the LNER and they will be paid:

        1) Goods trains at 1/3 proportion of receipts.
        2) For providing goods locos for shunting 15/10 per engine hour +
           2/- per guards hour.
        3) LNER to provide locos to work LTPB passenger trains from
           Rickmansworth at 25/- per engine hour.
        4) £39,050 for 18 Met locos and 27 wagons.

-Loan to the LNER any relevant LT staff with the option of their transfer back to the LT for training on electric trains.

-Convert Quainton Road to Verney Junction to single track.

-Widening: Bill given Royal assent on 2nd August 1935 and will form part of the 'New Works Programme' with the Government. Of this some £1,750,000 will be applicable to the Joint.

Watford Committee appoints a sub-committee to examine how the branch can be operated as economically as possible in light of the deficit for 1936 of £8,659.

1938

-Scrap 3 old Joint lorries and loan replacements from the LNER.

-Agreed to restore earlier deductions from wages.

-Approved to acquire land for improvements from the Post Office at Harrow.

-New Works 1935/40: all tenders approved.

-National Emergency: Staff joining His Majesties Services will be treated as being on leave for continuation of Company service in the context of pensions.

1939 Outbreak of Second War

-The original seal of the Joint was now worn out from use and it was agreed to replace it with one of the same design for £2 4s.

-New Works: Sir Richard McAlpine & Sons appointed as contractors for most bridge work between Harrow & Rickmansworth, except the bridges which will go to Horseley Bridge with Thomas Piggot Ltd. Due to the expected density of traffic and lack of refuge siding passing, loops will now be built at Chorley Wood and Chenies (!) at a cost of £33,600.

1940

-Ministry of Transport has assumed control of all the railways in the UK through the Railway Executive Ctte. In this the Joint is still considered a separate entity.

-New Works programme suspended until after the war. The value of these works held in suspense is £1,156,000 and some work would be undertaken to ensure that it could be left without serious deterioration.

-Annual income from rented property; 'north' = £1,008 at a cost of £250 and 'south' = £11,730 at a cost of £900.

-Pay increased plus war advance of 1s to 4s pw. Staff on service to have their service pay made up to their railway amount. Currently, some 27 staff have been called- up.

-Agreed to reduce the number of meetings of this and the Watford Committee to once per year with urgent matters being dealt with by Chairman's action.

Watford Committee: Permanent way staff 50% under strength. During the war track maintenance was at a basic level under the 'Essential Work Orders'.

1941

-For convenience during hostilities the management of the Joint would remain with the LTPB in 1942 and the accounts with the LNER.

-The Government Control Pool for the railways guarantees a minimum level of revenue and any excess will go to the parent companies. This minimum net revenue will be the average revenue for the Joint over the years 1935–7, which was £58,322. From this the LTPB will receive the first £5,500.

1942

-Agreed extra sidings at Quainton Road for the War Office and storage of food (£1,649). Most repair contacts postponed.

-Two further ticket collectors for Wendover to deal with Halton Camp traffic.

-Staff pensions will now be transferred into either the LPTB or LNER scheme, as appropriate, at a cost of £300.

-Permanent way: 'north' renewal by 57 yds and 'south' by 5,000 yds (£13,249).

-Dispose of inadequate crane (of 1898) at Harrow.

-Pay increases of £4,340 noted.

1943

-Agreed station Kiosk contracts 1) with Findlay & Co the tobacconists: 3 at Harrow, 1 each at N Harrow, Northwood & Rickmansworth at £559 pa, 2) with London Kiosks: 1 each at Harrow, Pinner, Northwood Hills, Moor Park, Rickmansworth & Gt. Missenden at £362 pa.

-Improve the loco water supply at Aylesbury because of extra goods traffic. Decided to get larger water mains and extra electric pumps at a cost of £1,097.

-Install 'Rolltic' automatic ticket issuing machines at Harrow (£315).

-Permanent Way: renewal 'north' 221 yds & 'south' about 5000 yds.

-Staff numbers: Met & Gc Jt. Weekly = 86 + Salaried = 249
                Watford Jt. Weekly = 12 + Salaried = 27   (thus total = 276)

-Agreed to extend petrol store at Chalfont & Latimer.

1944

-Agreed to install a siding at International Alloys near Aylesbury for the Ministry of Aircraft Production.(£2,500).

-Lengthen LNER down platform at Harrow from 420ft to 500ft in order to accommodate longer trains, which otherwise have to pick-up twice.

-Permanent Way: 'north' 1,178 yds & 'south' 6,035 yds (£12,381).

-Provide lavatory facilities for female staff.

1945

-Acquire a rapid printer for 'Rolltic' ticket machines at Harrow.

-Permanent Way: 'north' 1,336 yds & 'south' 1,365 yds (£15,700).

-Provide better washing and wc facilities at Harrow Yard.

-Poor water supply at Chesham so get National Fire Service to replenish the tank for £25 pw.

1946 End of the war

-Agreed repair of Aylesbury loco shed which is in danger of collapse. (£1,200).

-Approved LPTB use of the tip at Rickmansworth if they pay 6d/cu.yd for use of land, 6d/cu.yd for transport over the Joint line and also provide the necessary engines and stock.

-Responsibility for the Management & Accounts to continue as before.

-Proposed increase in fares.

-'Stop & proceed' working conditional upon installation of telephones at the signals.

-Revert to pre-war frequency of holding these meetings.

1947 Nationalisation

-The Transport Bill had been presented to Parliament on the 13th February 1947 that embraced the Joint. No compensation would be paid to the owners and the lease under which the Joint is to be demised, being merged into the freehold acquired by the British Transport Commission from the LPTB.

-Fares had risen during the war by 35%.

-Permanent Way renewal: 'north' 179 yds & 'south' 4m 1079 yds, (£3,000).

-Land slip ¼ m north of Moor Park to be repaired (£3,000).

-Joint 4t lorry at Aylesbury (AJ 12 of 1930) to be scrapped and replaced by a loan from LNER.

-Pay increases for staff of 396 will cost £21,737 in the year.

-Butler-Henderson of the LNER chaired the last meeting. During it, Lord Ashfield then resigned from the Joint and then from the LTPB Board upon his appointment to the British Transport Commission. The Joint Committee then thanked him for his services since 1932.

Thus at the end of 1947 the Joint came to an end after an separate existence of some 41 years.

ooooOOOoooo

The only item of rolling stock ever owned by the Joint was this 5 ton 'Accident' Hand Crane no.1. Built by Cowans Sheldon in 1914. It spent most of its life at Harrow and Northwood before being saved and restored at the Buckingham Railway Centre at Quainton Road, where many other items of Met & GC interest are preserved. *(C Foxell)*

The Croxley Rail Link

Proposed intermediate stations

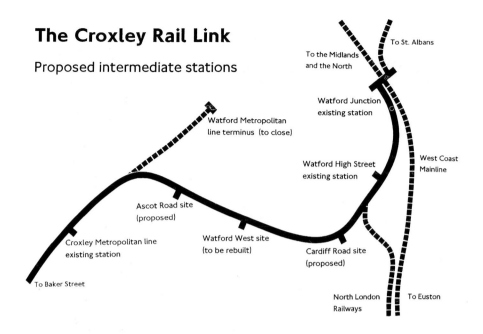

To St. Albans

To the Midlands
and the North

Watford Junction
existing station

Watford Metropolitan
line terminus (to close)

West Coast
Mainline

Watford High Street
existing station

Ascot Road site
(proposed)

Croxley Metropolitan line
existing station

Watford West site
(to be rebuilt)

Cardiff Road site
(proposed)

To Baker Street

North London
Railways

To Euston

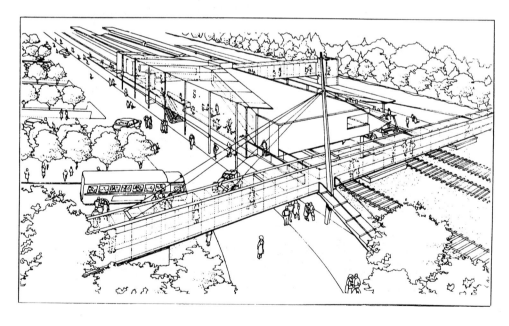

Top: the route of the suggested Croxley Rail Link and, Bottom: The proposed new
station at Rickmansworth on the site of the existing station car park (the old goods yard).

METRO. & L·N·E·RAILWAYS

CROXLEY

GOODS AND COAL DEPÔT

M
28½ ½
2
161 c 170

MET & GC JOINT COMMITTEE

TRESPASSERS WILL BE PROSECUTED.

PENALTY FORTY SHILLING OR

IMPRISONMENT FOR ONE MONTH.

METROPOLITAN & GREAT CENTRAL
– JOINT COMMITTEE Nº 1 –
TO BE RETURNED TO NORTHWOOD

A selection of Joint signs, including milepost 28½ near Gt. Missenden which marked the dividing point of maintenance responsibility and the plate of hand crane no.1. *(CAF)*

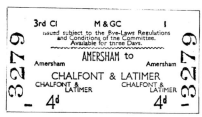

A selection of Joint ephemera including at mid-left a rare Met Pullman ticket of 1926.
(Bob Clark, Richard Hardy, Frank Bunker & Clive Foxell)

APPENDIX 2

THE Met & GCR AGREEMENTS

In 1925 the Met sought advice from Counsel on the interpretation of the existing Agreements, in relation to the division of receipts from the Joint with the LNER. The following is a **précis** of the legal background to the Agreements, prepared by the Met as briefing for Counsel and it provides a useful summary of the evolution of the Agreements.

In 1872 Sir Edward Watkin who was then Chairman of the MS&LR became Chairman & Managing Director of the Met and continued to be Chairman of both companies until 1894. So long as he had controlling influence over the policy of the two companies their relations were close and friendly and gradually extensions were made of the Met in a northerly direction and the MS&LR in the southerly direction. In the autumn of 1890 the MS&LR deposited a Bill for a line from Annesley to Quainton Road. The application to Parliament in the session of 1891 was unsuccessful, but a Bill introduced in the next session became the MS&LR (Extension to London) Act 1893 whereby they obtained powers to construct the line to Quainton Road. This as approved by Parliament differed from the original proposal in that the MS&LR were authorised to build an independent terminus at Marylebone (instead of depending on Baker Street station of the Met) and a railway to Marylebone from a junction with the Met at Canfield Place, near Finchley Road.

In view of this extension the two companies had earlier entered into an Agreement of 18/12/1890 giving the MS&LR running powers over the Met from Quainton Road to Baker Street. This subject to the restriction that the MS&LR should not, without consent of the Met, take up any passenger or other traffic passing between any two places on the Met and subject to other provisions of the Agreement, which include payment to the Met of 66 2/3% of mileage receipts from all traffic over the Met by virtue of the running powers.

In the Session of 1895 the MS&LR introduced a Bill to authorise a Railway from a junction with the Met south of Harrow to Canfield Place with the MS&LR, authorised in 1893. This was practically a widening of the Met, who opposed the Bill, and as a result an Agreement between the two dated 28/6/95 was confirmed by the MS&LR Act of 1895 which provided that the Met should construct this Railway and that the MS&LR should have exclusive and separate use of it.

In 1898 the GWR obtained authority to construct a Railway from a junction with their main line near Acton to High Wycombe by the junction with their Wycombe Railway. In 1898 the Great Central Railway (ex MS&LR) obtained authority to construct a Railway from the GWR line above from Northolt Junction to Neasden. By the GW & GC Railways Act of 1899 the GWR line from Northolt and Princes Risboro' became a joint railway and an extension north to Ashendon Junction was authorised to be built by them. A further extension to the GCR mainline at Grendon Underwood was also authorised to be built by the GCR so that it obtained an entirely new route to London as an alternative to that over the Met from Quainton Road

By the GCR Act of 1907 the GWR lines from Princes Risboro' and Aylesbury are vested in the GW & GC Joint Committee. The Bill for the GW&GC Railways Act of 1899 was strongly opposed by the Met, but the Bill became an Act with a section for the protection of the Met:-

1) -the two Companies shall pay the Met compensation for their outlay incurred between Quainton Road & Canfield Place, not necessary for providing for the GCR traffic, as to be settled by arbitration under the Act of 1889.

2) -in estimating the outlay to be paid by the two companies there shall be deducted that representing the value to the Met of the land & works.

As the compensation could not be agreed the determination was referred to Lord Robertson as arbitrator but in due course the parties came to a settlement expressed in Heads of Agreement which became incorporated in the Met & GC Act of 1905.

This made a considerable change to the relations between them inasmuch as, excluding the Met branch to Uxbridge:-

1) -the Met railway from Canfield Place to Harrow South Junction over which the GCR would have exclusive running powers under the Agreement of 1890, was to be leased to the GCR for 999 years and

2) -the Met line from Harrow South Junction to Verney Junction, with the Chesham branch was leased to for 999 years to a Met & GC Joint Committee as constituted by the Met & GCR Companies' Act 1905.

The Heads provided that a formal Agreement be entered into but the settlement of this provoked many questions and disputes and an arbitration was embodied in the Agreement of 11/6/1913. As Counsel is aware, the LNER are the successors of the GCR as a result of the amalgamation under the Railways Act of 1921.

We now turn to consideration of Article 26 of the Agreement of 11/6/1913 and it is necessary to appreciate the position in 1904 prior to the Heads of Agreement. Running powers were given by the Agreement of 18/10/1890 to the GCR over the Met from Quainton Road to Baker Street, but were restricted without consent from taking up passengers/traffic between any two Met stations. Thus a GCR main line train could stop and pick up passengers at a Met station north of Harrow, but was then bound to run without stop to Marylebone. However the Met did permit the GCR to run a small number of Marylebone trains to serve Met stations north of Harrow. When terms were discussed between the two companies for making them equal partners in the Joint line, the Met required some guarantee against their loss of traffic in respect of their railways south of Harrow, by reason of the GCR competing for traffic to & from the Joint line. Consequently a pooling arrangement was given effect in the Agreement of 11/6/1913. However differences in the meaning of this between the two went to Arbitration by Mr Ernest Moon QC and his award is in the formal Agreement. *(see Chapter 5)*

The Met believes the phraseology to be ambiguous in that it intended that they would be compensated for the whole of their loss due to the diverted traffic not just only 66 2/3%. *(Detailed calculations are then given for the effect of a overall deficit in 1912 and a surplus in 1913)* However the Arbitrator accepted the views of the GCR and added to the agreement the words "less 33 1/3% thereof", of the pool for working each company working its own traffic. Nevertheless the Met has continued to believe that the meaning is open to doubt but cannot now be questioned. But Counsel will observe that this has a very curious result, namely that the energetic partner is prejudiced, while the slothful partner profits by its sloth and the energy of the other partner, since the partner who expends capital to improve its line receives no consideration under the Agreement.

Now this bears hardly on the Met who have recently expended large sums in improving their line *i.e.* the costly doubling of their line between Finchley Road and Wembley (1915) which has increased traffic considerably. Again the Met have at their own cost electrified the Joint line from Harrow to Rickmansworth giving an improved service. The result of this has been to increase Met receipts so that it will probably be a greater contributor to the pool. On the other hand the GCR/LNER have not taken any steps to enhance their traffic by capital improvements and prefer to leave the development of the line to their more energetic partner.

The opinion of Counsel is sought firstly on this issue as to whether this additional traffic resulting from these improvements can be excluded from the Joint pool of receipts. Secondly, the Met has come to the conclusion that to enhance traffic they must construct a relief line from of their existing line near Willesden Green, passing under and down the Edgware Road to join the Met Inner Circle line at Edgware Road station. In this case must such traffic be brought into the Joint pool? As the third point the Met suggests that a strict interpretation of the Agreement would exclude traffic originating or terminating at Baker Street Station. Since the words in the Agreement are not to & from Baker Street **or** the stations on the Inner Circle, but to & from Baker Street **and** the stations on the Inner Circle.

In his Opinion of the 9/11/1925 the Counsel, A C Clauson of Lincoln's Inn gave the view that in respect of point: -
1)   The Met at the date of the Agreement ran between Baker Street & Harrow South Junction and the expression includes all alterations and widenings referred to.
2)   Such a relief line would make it necessary to account to the pool for receipts accruing between Willesden Green and Harrow South, but not between Edgware Road and Willesden Green.
3)   Passenger train traffic originating or terminating at Baker Street comes within the meaning of the Agreement. It does not appear that the receipts can be confined to traffic to and from Inner Circle stations through Baker Street, so as to exclude traffic to and from Baker Street itself.

Thus the Met got little comfort from this legal exercise. Mr I Buchanan Pritchard, who prepared the brief for the Met, subsequently joined the LNER as their legal advisor (!)

APPENDIX 3

FINANCIAL PERSPECTIVES

In a sense the Joint was free-standing company and thus presented its own accounts. Incomes from passenger and goods traffic as well as that from rental (land, buildings and commercial sites) were set by a broad competitive environment. On the other hand, costs were related to labour and infrastructure investment, plus financial overheads. In this respect the owners of the Joint were not well placed having both inherited the aftermath of the high costs of their construction. The MS&LR route had dramatically exceeded the budget and delayed income, to be later compounded by the costs of Watkin's London Extension. In contrast its partner the Met, was initially inundated with passengers but suffered from financial malpractice before Watkin arrived. Although his battles with John Forbes and construction of the Extension were expensive, he managed to pay moderate dividends helped by the income from property and other holdings. Afterwards the reign of Selbie was characterised by lower dividends as a result of the cost of electrification and factors common to all railways such as the First War, the General Strike and increasing competition from motor vehicles.

It was common practice in Victorian times to pay dividends during the construction phase. Both companies had 'avoided the evil day' by continuing to raise fresh finance whilst paying dividends out of their existing capital to try and keep the shareholders happy. This was made possible by issuing of preference shares and debentures, as bait. Although this imprudent approach was not uncommon, it was the scale that in the longer term added to their ongoing financial burden. When Watkin arrived on the railway scene he created a financial smoke screen and then made it worse by embarking on his massive investment to bring about his vision.

From our present perspective it is difficult to judge the viability of the Met and the GCR, as owners of the Joint, whose financial positions had ramifications for that company. The accounting conventions of the Victorian and Edwardian era were different and more lax than our own in which items such as the treatment of depreciation, work in progress and the allocation of overheads were susceptible to 'creative accounting'. Equally the evaluation of what is 'good' or 'bad' performance changes with time, with varying emphasis on growth, dividend income and potential. Overlaying this assessment is the 'sentiment' of the Stock Market towards a particular sector, which in this case was known as 'Home Rails'. During the early years optimism drove shares to unsustainable levels until the bubble burst around 1849 and then as railways matured their stock became a safe 'blue chip' investment for many. However, as railway competition increased and road transport developed, 'Home Rails' steadily declined.

The fortunes of the MS&LR and its successor the GCR were parodied at the time as 'Money Sunk & Lost' and 'Gone Completely', however some more recent studies have presented a more considered assessment. On one hand Messrs Emblin, Longbone & Jackson point out that the inevitably costly expansion of the Met and GWR London Extensions, as well as the improved facilities on the East-West coast route were essential to the survival, profit and growth of the GCR. Although these created a debt which had to be serviced, it was not true that the GCR never paid a dividend, indeed the majority of shares were 'non-contingent' and dividends were paid on most of these. After Watkin, the excellent management team led by Henderson exploited the earlier massive investment and the authors point out that although the finances of the GCR were never robust, they were not greatly dissimilar to the rest of the 'Home Rails'. Equally, when 'grouping' was inevitable in 1923, the GCR became a valued constituent of the LNER.

By contrast Messrs Bloxsom & Hendry trace the origins of the GCR problems to the ongoing crippling debt incurred by the SA&M and exacerbated by the schemes of the MS&L and the GCR. The consequent capital structure of the companies drained profits into the preference dividends leaving an inherent financial weakness that led to merger negotiations in the early 1900's, but ended in failure. However 'Grouping' overtook these talks and in the resulting LNER the fragility of the GCR was counterbalanced by the more prosperous NER.

The 'truth' probably lies between these two viewpoints but from our current interest in the Joint the essential factor is that the debt/dividend considerations meant that any transfer charges were loaded and GCR investment was not a priority in what they saw as a Met commuter line. Equally the Met under Seblie had to 'run a tight ship' to the extent that LT complained that the Met infrastructure was inferior to their own network. This all led to a prudent culture in the Joint in which all expenditure was carefully vetted and where the partners were suspicious of any spend favouring the operations of the other party. Against this background it is appropriate to turn to the reported financial performance of the Joint. In the following table, which has been constructed from available accounts, the headings have been recast in an attempt to produce comparable figures. These have been rounded to the nearest Pound (£) and therefore there may be some small inconsistencies. Nevertheless it shows some interesting features and trends in passenger and goods traffic. In 1913 the net revenue was split between the Met & the GCR, but as a result of negotiation the accounts for1923 onward show a preferential profit of £5,000 for the Met before the sharing.

The financial significance of Joint to the respective partners can be crudely shown by comparing a typical profit for each from the Joint in the early 1920's of about £40,000 with the overall profit of the GCR of around £2M and the Met some £800,000. However the transit traffic was more valuable to both.

MET & GC JT. COMMITTEE REVENUE ACCOUNTS (£)

Year	1913	1922	1924	1925	1936	1937
RECEIPTS						
Passenger						
First	7,829	16,261	) 174,161	) 162,682	7,012	7,999
Third	75,948	101,475	)inc. third	)inc. third	113,047	118,343
Season	13,755	48,445	52,042	52,350	68,113	71,673
Workmen	294	715	867	1,191	6.603	6,948
Parcels/mail	40,092	57,281	57,165	61,410	72,459	61,663
Total	137,920	281,177	284,235	277,633	267,234	266,619
Goods						
Merchandise(2)	24,683	47,622	27,023	32,573	23,364	24,800
Livestock	1,000	2,036	1,610	2,360	844	83
Coal etc.	19,814	33,914	40,242	38,462	41,362	41,012
Other minerals	10,140	22,102	35,204	31,612	15,510	8,776
Misc.	870	2,659	1,821	1,742	3,921	5,022
Total op. revenue	56,508	108,334	105,900	106,749	83,627	79,693
Rents & other receipts	7,061	10,446	13,187	13,077	14,171	13,819
TOTAL	**210,490**	**399,957**	**403,322**	**397,459**	**366,406**	**360,131**
EXPENDITURE						
Permanent way	31,813	80,153	71,761	63,782	63771	64,449
Shunting loco exp.	2,812	11,667	12,701	11,933	8,971	9,971
Traffic expenses	20,108	62,286	58,445	60,882	(o)58,243	59,485
Legal/rent etc.	7,249	4,877	13,857	13,677	15,638	15,316
Running powers	58,643	120,684	117,738	(¹)112,898	110,628	113,431
Misc.	27	117	115	110	------	------
Total op. exp.	120,652	289,784	274,617	263,282	257,211	262,652
Interest, rentals & fixed charges(3)	51,734	51,735	46,237	46,237	45,723	45,635
TOTAL	**172,386**	**341,519**	**320,854**	**309,519**	**302,934**	**308,287**
NET REVENUE TO SHARE	**29,104**	**29,219**	**82,468**	**87,940**	**63,472**	**51,844**

Notes: (o) including salaries of £42,275.

(1) passenger: Met = £34,353 + LNER = £55,823

goods: Met = £19,252 + LNER = £3,420

(2) net of delivery costs.

(3) including rent of leased lines i.e.Met & GC Jnt of £44,000 + O&AT of £600.
The above figures include the reported profit/loss for the Watford branch, which
in: 1936= - £8,659: '37= - £7,612: '38= - £7,467: '39= - £10,465: '40= £51,099:
'41= £73,157: '42= £32,916: '43= 57,512: '44= £36,897: '45= £41,861: '46=
£43,028: '47= £39,176.

APPENDIX 3

'JOINT' STATISTICS

TRACK LENGTH

Overall length of Joint = 48½miles, including Chesham branch (4miles), Watford branch (2miles 37chains) and the moiety of Aylesbury Joint station.

STAFF NUMBERS

In 1906 = 181, in 1947 = 396

FARES		
	1914	1d per mile
	1917	1.5d: to discourage wartime travel.
	1920	1.75d
	1923	1.5d: upon grouping.
	1937	1.575d
	1947	2.5d: postwar

TRAFFIC IN 1925

Engine Mileage
Steam:

	Coaching:	Met	322,581
		LNE	588,674
	Goods	Met	149,620
		LNE	19,746
Electric:		Met	224,300
	Total miles		1,304,951

Passenger Numbers

Originating on Joint = 3,512,993   Total = 13,016,999

Goods

	Originating on Joint	Total
Merchandise	15,370	140,772
Coal etc.	756	328,440
Other minerals	63,162	285,220
Total tons	79,288	754,432
Livestock numbers	27,177	40,172

STATIONS

Name	Opened	Changes
Harrow on the Hill	2 Aug 1880	
North Harrow Halt	22 Mar 1915	North Harrow 1928
Pinner	1 May 1885	
Northwood Hills	13 Nov 1933	
Northwood	1 Sept 1887	
Sandy Lodge	9 Apr 1910	Moor Park & Sandy Lodge 18/10/1923: Moor Park 1958
--Croxley Green	2 Nov 1925	
--Watford	2 Nov 1925	
Rickmansworth	1 Sept 1887	
Chorley Wood	8 Jul 1889	*Chorley Road in some 1889 documents:* Chorley Wood & Chenies1915: Chorley Wood 1958: Chorleywood 1961
Chalfont Road	8 Jul 1889	Chalfont & Latimer 20/11/1915
--Chesham	8 Jul 1889	
Amersham	1 Sep 1892	Amersham 1920: Amersham & Chesham Bois 1922: Amersham 1939
Great Missenden	1 Sept 1892	
Wendover	1 Sept 1892	
Stoke Mandeville	1 Sept 1892	
Aylesbury (Town)	GWR 20/10/1863 A&BR 23/9/1868 Met 1/9/1892	
Waddesdon Manor	1 Jan 1897	Waddesdon 1/10/1922: closed 4/7/1936
Quainton Road	23 Sept 1868	Closed pass. 4/3/1963, goods 7/1966
--Waddesdon	1 April 1871	Waddesdon Road 1/10/1922 Closed 30/11/1935
--Westcott	1 April 1871	Closed 30/11/1935
--Wotton	1 April 1871	Closed 30/11/1935
--Wood Siding	1 April 1871	Closed 30/11/1935
-- Brill	March 1872	Closed 30/11/1935
Grandborough Road	23 Sept 1868	Granborough Road 6/10/20 Closed pass. 4/7/1936
Winslow Road	23 Sept 1868	Closed pass. 4/7/1936
Verney Junction (Met)	23 Sept 1868	Closed pass. 4/7/1936, goods 6/9/1947

MILEPOSTS

GCR/LNER: located on the up side, from zero at Manchester (London Road). Met/LT: from Harrow to Quainton Road, downside, from zero at Baker Street. 'South' refers to south of mp 28½ etc.

GOODS SERVICES: 1931 Weekdays

a) LNER

Down: MB(02.50) - HH(03.27)
        QR(11.55) - WD
        QR(20.10) - WD
        MB(22.15) - HH(22.32)

Up: HH(04.25) - Neasden,LNER
     WD(03.00) - QR(04.04)
     HH(23.40) - MB
     WD(03.25) - QR(07.16)

b) Met (excluding various shunting, elec. loco movements south of Neasden & Chesham branch goods with 'shuttle'. Some trains called at any station as requested.)

Train no.

1 down FR(03.45)-HH -C&L-all to QR-VJ(14.00)
  up   VJ(15.50)-QR-AYL-WR-GM-C&L-RW-all-HH-WG-Neasden(02.18)
2 down FR(05.25)-HH-PN-RW-all to VJ(19.02)
  up   VJ(08.25)-QR-GM-HH-Neasden, Met(12.31)
2a down ND(04.30)-HH-WAT-RW(06.14)
3 down FR(21.17)-WG-ND-HH-RW-C&L-AYL-QR-VJ(06.10)
  up   VJ(08.10)-all to C&L-RW-WAT-PN-HH-Neasden, Met(23.08)
4 down ND(19.30)-HH-AYL-QR(22.15)
  up   QR(23.25)-AYL-HH-Neasden, Met(03.15)
5 down ND(01.05)-AYL-QR(03.45)
  up   QR(05.)-AYL-RW-WAT-NW-HH-WP-ND(12.23)
6 down Light engine & brake van: ND(Met)(03.10)-HH-WE-AYL(05.07)
  up   VJ(00.10)-QR-(00.55) to BRILL
  up   VJ(13.50)-AYL-RW-HH-WP-Neasden, Met(15.10)
8 down ND(05.10)-HH-HILL-UX(06.43)
  up   UX(08.42)-RP-RL-HH(10.49)
  down HH(10.59)-GWS(11.10)
  up   GWS(11.33)-HH-WP-ND-WG- Neasden, Met(14.41)
10 down ND(07.38)-HH-NW-WSJ-RW-C&L-CH(14.22)
  up   CH(16.25)-ND(17.19)
11 down FR(06.50)-WG(shunt yard)-Neasden, Met(10.37)
12 down ND(03.25)-HH-WE-AYL(05.07)
  up   AYL(01.50)-C&L-HH-Neasden, Met(03.50)
15 down Light engine & brake van: ND(Met)(10.34)-VJ(12.21)
  up   VJ(13.50)-AYL-RW-ND(17.06)

Key: AYL= Aylesbury, C&L= Chalfont&Latimer, CH= Chesham, CW= Chorley Wood, FR= Finchley Road, GSW= Gas Works siding (S.Harrow), HILL= Hillingdon, HH=Harrow, MB=Marylebone ND=Neasden, NW=Northwood, PN=Pinner, QR=Quainton Rd., RW=Rickm'th, SM=Stoke Mandeville, RL= Rayners Lane, RP=Ruislip, UX=Uxbridge, VJ=Verney Junction, WAT=Watford, WD=Woodford, WE=Wendover, WG=Willesden Green, WP=Wembley Park, WSJ=Watford South Junction.

PASSENGER TRAIN JOURNEY TIMES (Best times in minutes)[1]

Date[3]	1903	1920	1931	1939	1958	1980	2000
From Marylebone to:-							
9.3 m Harrow	15	14	14	12	14	12	11
17.2 m Rickmansworth	--	29	26	27	27	24	21
23.6 m Amersham	--	54	39	46	42	35	29
37.4 m Aylesbury	53	53	52	48	59	58	49
44.3 m Quainton Road	--	83	74	79	96	--	--
50.3 m Verney Junction	--	106	96	--	--	--	--
From Baker St. to:-							
Harrow	25	19	15	15	17	16	16
Rickmansworth	42	30	30	26	31	27.5	28
18.5m Watford	--	--[2]	33	33	39	40	37
Amersham	59	45	53	48	50	39.5	40
Aylesbury	87	84	72	79	80	--	--
Quainton Road	100	90	101	90	--	--	--
Verney Junction	119	120	131	--	--	--	--

(1) The 'best times' for each date often reflects different trains i.e. fast v stopping.
(2) The Watford branch opened in 1925, with an Met service of 40 trains/day taking 35 mins to Baker St. and briefly an LNER service of 30 trains/day to Marylebone.
(3) Baker St. trains:
Met steam haulage beyond Harrow until 1925 and thence from Rickmansworth after electrification. LT continued with LNER locos until electrification to Amersham in 1961. This became the terminus for LT trains.
  Marylebone trains:
Steam hauled by the GCR until 1923, thence by LNER to 1947 and after by BR until they introduced DMU's in 1960. From 1992 the Chiltern Turbo's took over.

TRAIN FREQUENCY (typical no. down trains on a weekday)

Date[3]	1903	1920	1931	1939	1958	1980	2000
No. of down trains per weekday beyond Rickmansworth.							
GC/LNE/BR/Chiltern	17	23	25	28	22	19	33
Met/LT	22	23	20	28	33	33	56
No. of down trains per weekday to Watford.							
Met/LT	--	--[2]	45	54	55	69	83

PRIMARY SOURCES

The main archives relating to the 'Joint' have been transferred from the British Rail Archives to the London Metropolitan Archive at 40 Northampton Road, London EC1R 0HB and the following from Accession No. 1297 have been referred to in researching this book:

MGCJ 1/1	Joint Committee Minutes (written).	1906-17
MGCJ 1/2	Joint Committee Minutes (written).	1917-33
MGCJ 1/3	Joint Committee Minutes (written).	1933-48
MGCJ 1/4	Joint Committee Minutes (printed).	1906-11
MGCJ 1/5	Joint Committee Minutes (printed).	1911-22
MGCJ 1/6	Officers Conference Minutes (printed).	1906-13
MGCJ 1/7	Officers Conference Minutes (printed).	1914-36
MGCJ 1/8	Oxford & Aylesbury Tramway Co. papers.	1899-1905
MGCJ 3/1	Litho. plans of the Met & GC Joint Line.	1907
MET 3/1	MS&LR and Met Agreements.	1894-1913
MET 3/3	Acquisition of the A&BR by the Met.	1899
MET 4/8	GCR use of the Met lines.	1894-98
MET 4/11&13	Collection of Met printed matter & photos.	----
MET 10 /39	St. John's Wood Railway widening.	1865-78
MET 10/42	Extension from Pinner to Rickmansworth.	1885
MET 10/47	Extension from Rickmansworth to Chesham.	1889
MET 10/54	Proposed extension to High Wycombe.	1892-96
MET 10/112	Alterations to Harrow station.	1907-8
MET 10/126	Crash at Aylesbury station.	1904
MET 10/127	Met Pullman cars.	1909-22
MET 10/230	Watford branch opening.	1925
MET 10/378	Advice from Counsel.	1925
MET 10/535	Opening to Aylesbury.	1892
MET 10/543	Goods working.	1927
MET 10/656	Trials MS&LR locomotives.	1897
MET 10/659	SER, MS&LR and Met Agreements.	1889-90
MET 10/700	Temporary MS&LR junction near West Hampstead.	1895
MET 10/705	Discussions on division of receipts with LNER.	1923
MET 10/708	Watford branch correspondence.	1931
MET 10/709	MS&LR and Met letters on gradients & clearances.	1897-8
MET 10/711	Proposed extension to 'Central England'.	1889
MET 10/712	Alterations to Harrow station.	1928-33
MET 10/727	Speed of GCR trains.	1904
MET 10/758	LT Bill.	1932
MET 15/1	Absorption of Met staff by the LTPB.	1928-33
MET 19/1	Guide to the Extension.	----
WAT 1/1	Watford Joint Committee Minutes.	1926-47

Plus various public & working timetables, railway's publications, local newspapers & other records.

SECONDARY SOURCES

C J Allen	The Locomotive Exchanges	
	Ian Allan	1949
R M G Baker	The Metropolitan & Great Central Joint Line	
	Railway Magazine June p360 & July p501	1960
M Bloxsom & R Hendry	Great Central -The Real Problem	
	Back Track Vol 10 p266	1996
J Graeme Bruce	Steam To Silver	
	London Transport	1970
Tony Coldwell	The Halton Light Railway	
	Private publication (Wendover Lib. ref.L442:38)	1992
F Cockman	The Railways of Buckinghamshire	
	Private publication (Bucks Record Office)	1971
F Cockman	The Railway Era in Buckinghamshire	
	Records of Buckinghamshire Vol 19 pt2 p165	1972
George Dow	The First Railway Between Manchester & Sheffield	
	LNER	1945
George Dow	The Great Central	
	Locomotive Publishing Co.	1959
R Emblin, B Longbone	Money Sunk & Lost	
& D Jackson	Back Track Vol 9 p129	1995
C Hamilton Ellis	British Railway History	
	Allen & Unwin	1954
E J S Gadsden	The Duke of Buckingham's Railways	
	Private publication (Bucks Reference Library)	1962
Frank Goudie	Metropolitan Steam	
	Roundhouse Books	1963
Frank Goudie	The Aylesbury & Buckingham Railway	
	British Railway Journal no.64 p267	1999
Alan A Jackson	London's Metropolitan Railway	
	David & Charles	1986
David Jackson	J G Robinson - A Lifetime's Work	
	Oakwood Press	1996
O S Nock	The Woodhead Tunnel – (in The Railway-Lover's	
	Companion) Eyre & Spottiswoode	1963
L T C Rolt	The Making of a Railway	
	Sutton Publishing	1971
J de Rothschild	The Rothschilds of Waddesdon Manor	
	Collins	1979
Robert Robotham	Great Central Railway's London Extension	
	Ian Allan	1999
Bill Simpson	The Brill Tramway	
	Oxford Publishing Co.	1985

The end of the line. During the last days of Verney Junction a station man with some time to spare created this striking garden display on one of the station platforms. Perhaps these figures represent the beautiful sirens called up by The Duke of Buckingham and Sir Harry Verney that lured the great Sir Edward Watkin to lose his way in the Vale of Aylesbury? *(H C Casserley)*

Inside Rear Cover, top: The ubiquitous brown multiple-electric T stock were the mainstay of the Met 'all-stations' and semi-fast services over the Joint, whilst the Bo-Bo electric locos with the Dreadnought coaches operated the fast trains. This picture shows examples towards the end of their lives in 1960, with the T stock by the up platform at Rickmansworth beside Bo-Bo no.11 'George Romney' which is arriving with the Aylesbury-bound train, ready for the changeover to steam traction for the rest of the journey. *(Colour-Rail LT32/ B. Patton)*

Inside Rear Cover, bottom: A picture that symbolises the era of the diesel on the Joint. Taken in brilliant weather in the March of 1989 it shows the beginning of the BR improvements, with new liveries and refurbished stations, that would culminate in the operation of Chiltern Railways. At Stoke Mandeville a Marylebone bound type 115 DMU in new Network-Southeast colours waits in he station, whilst a type 47 diesel no.47613 approaches with an engineering ballast train. *(Ron Potter)*

Rear Cover, top: In the last phase of steam operation over the Joint as a BR(M) rebuilt class 7P 4-6-0 no.46112 'Sherwood Forester' leaves Amersham in the winter of1963. Hauling the ex-12.38 from Marylebone and destined for Nottingham it makes a striking scene of sun, steam and Chiltern snow some 400ft above sea level. *(Colour-Rail BRM408/ J.P.Mallett)*

Rear Cover, bottom: The 'Steam on the Met' events often provided a memorable contrast of the old and the new on the Joint. Here during the May 1998 programme, a modern Chiltern Railways type 165 turbo diesel service train approaches Amersham station from the south. It emerges through the billowing smoke and steam of a preserved ex-LNER Thompson designed class B1 4-6-0 no.1264, which worked on the Joint over 50 years ago. *(Ron Potter)*